FINISH

LINE

FINISH

LINE

DISPELLING FEAR, FINDING PEACE,
AND PREPARING *for the* END OF YOUR LIFE

ROBERT WOLGEMUTH

ZONDERVAN
BOOKS

ZONDERVAN BOOKS

Finish Line
Copyright © 2023 by Robert Wolgemuth

Requests for information should be addressed to:
Zondervan, *3900 Sparks Dr. SE, Grand Rapids, Michigan 49546*

Zondervan titles may be purchased in bulk for educational, business, fundraising, or sales promotional use. For information, please email SpecialMarkets@Zondervan.com.

ISBN 978-0-310-36492-4 (audio)

Library of Congress Cataloging-in-Publication Data

Names: Wolgemuth, Robert D., author.
Title: Finish line : dispelling fear, finding peace, and preparing for the end of your life / Robert Wolgemuth.
Description: Grand Rapids : Zondervan, 2023. | Summary: "Finish Line by acclaimed author and speaker Robert Wolgemuth is a spiritual and practical guide to approaching the end of your life not with confusion but with clarity, inspiring you to live well now, not with fear but with anticipation and joy"— Provided by publisher.
Identifiers: LCCN 2022032490 (print) | LCCN 2022032491 (ebook) | ISBN 9780310364894 (hardcover) | ISBN 9780310364917 (ebook)
Subjects: LCSH: Death—Religious aspects—Christianity. | Death—Psychological aspects. | BISAC: RELIGION / Christian Living / Personal Growth | FAMILY & RELATIONSHIPS / Life Stages / Later Years
Classification: LCC BT825 .W65 2023 (print) | LCC BT825 (ebook) | DDC 236/.1—dc23/eng/20221123
LC record available at https://lccn.loc.gov/2022032490
LC ebook record available at https://lccn.loc.gov/2022032491

Cover design: Studio Gearbox
Cover illustrations: Marish / Shutterstock
Interior design: Sara Colley

Printed in the United States of America

22 23 24 25 26 LBC 5 4 3 2 1

To Nancy—
thank you for saying "I do" to a man
ten years chronologically closer to
his finish line than you are,
loving him well, and embracing the undeniable
challenges this would mean. You are God's
gift of grace in human loveliness.

CONTENTS

BEFORE YOU BEGIN

S o, Joni, do you ever wonder what it'll be like, crossing from this life into the next?"

I'm asked that a lot. Look, I'm a quadriplegic who's lived in a wheelchair for more than fifty-five years. I'm straining with head back, arms wide, and pumping everything I've got into that photo finish at the tape. Do I wonder what that moment will be like? You bet I do.

What I am about to say is not really biblical, but here's how I like to picture it. I see myself bursting across the finish line and—like a marathoner—collapsing on hands and knees. I sink my hands into the sands of that celestial shore, heaving, sweating, and gasping. "I made it . . . I made it . . . I can't believe I made it!" Then I roll over on my back and lie still with eyes closed, letting the restful sound of the gentle waves and the wind wash over me.

In the quiet, I feel the presence of Someone standing above me, Someone in whose cool shadow I feel bathed and blessed. I open my eyes and see . . . Jesus. His head is eclipsing the sun. He smiles down at me and offers His hand, as would any friend. I take it happily, and in one swift motion He pulls me up.

"Welcome home, sweetheart," He whispers as he looks admiringly at me with unimaginably kind eyes. Then he pulls me close and pat-pats my back like Daddy used to do. "It's been hard and long, but you're safe now," He says, patting me some more. At this point, I am sobbing until He holds me an arm's length away. I blink twice, for he almost looks like my Daddy, or maybe my Brother. Or Lover. Or King.

"You made me look so *good* back there on earth," He says.

My immediate reaction? Drop to my knees and kiss His feet. But the dream dissipates. The reality of what will then actually happen takes over. And although the details are cloaked in mystery, the Bible describes a glorious dénouement with angels and rewards; the devil and his hordes—all of them—destroyed; death gone; Christ's name vindicated as He is crowned the undisputed King of the universe. The Bible says we will reign alongside Him, spreading His kingdom of love, light, and beauty throughout the endless cosmos. Our song of suffering will be over, and forever we will sing of Jesus' sufferings and how his excruciatingly tender love won for us so great a salvation.

In a crude nutshell, that's what happens on the other side of the finish line. In light of all this, I ask you, *Don't you want to make the most of life in the home stretch?*

My friend Robert Wolgemuth sure does. We are close friends, and for the decades I've known him, I've never seen this man fritter away his time, treasure, or talents. He understands that life is an unspeakably precious gift, and as such, he stewards carefully the twenty-four-hour slices of time with which he has been blessed. Robert is my kind of brother in Christ—he's feeling his stride on his last lap, drawing on his second wind, and investing heavily in what lies beyond the tape at the finish.

My friend has spent years thinking about eternal ROIs and how everything a Christian does here on earth has a direct bearing on their capacity for joy, worship, and service in Heaven. Earth is Robert's minor league warm-up for the major leagues up there. And because he is such a great manager of life's gifts, he's my choice to author a book called *Finish Line*.

And he's covered *everything*. Just run your finger down the topics in the table of contents and you'll agree that Robert is a man who can show you how to put your house in order. Consider him your "close of life" coach, providing tips and tools that cover just about every question you might have about finishing the race of life well. My friend is a great writer and has made his chapters inspiring, easy to grasp, and practical.

But Robert has also written *Finish Line* as a challenge. He esteems you, his reader, as a Philippians 3:12 kind of believer who genuinely wants to press on to take hold of that for which Christ Jesus took hold of you:

> Not that I have already obtained all this, or have already arrived at my goal, but I press on to take hold of that for which Christ Jesus took hold of me.

The volume you hold in your hands is your playbook, helping you strive toward the goal to win the prize for which God has called you heavenward.

So if you're wondering how to flesh out these words from Philippians in a practical way—especially if you're in the home stretch, as the apostle Paul was—Robert can show you. Find a comfortable chair and a pen and highlighter and let him cheer you on from the sidelines as you press on toward the finish line. Your finish line.

You don't want to miss *anything* on the other side of that finish line tape.

JONI EARECKSON TADA,
Joni and Friends International Disability Center,
Agoura, California

PREFACE

SEEDS PLANTED

*Whether you stand or walk on the moving sidewalk at
the airport, you're eventually going to get to the end.*

ME . . . A TRAVELER

The Orlando funeral service was finished. Almost two hours of memories, tears, tributes, hymn singing, laughter, and a gospel message were in the books. It was time to show a video I had spontaneously shot one morning from the balcony of our home.[1]

Everyone watched the screen as a woman—Bobbie—walked from left to right. Striding on a neighborhood street, her stature was upright and confident, even though she was only a few weeks away from her death. The people in the audience could hear her singing.

---

1. I shot this with my phone early one morning. Bobbie did not know I was recording it. My friend and film producer David Nixon put it together for us.

When we walk with the Lord in the light of His Word,
What a glory He sheds on our way!
While we do His good will, He abides with us still,
And with all who will trust and obey.[2]

At the close of the video, the screen went black and these words appeared in white letters:

"Unless a kernel of wheat falls to the ground and dies, it remains only a single seed. But if it dies, it produces many seeds." (John 12:24)[3]

A sweet reverence filled the air. Just a moment of quiet, then Dr. David Swanson, my pastor, asked the congregation to stand. The funeral director and his associate walked down the middle aisle toward the coffin that had been centered in the nave, gently pivoted, and wheeled it out of the sanctuary. Dr. Swanson then invited the family, seated in the first several pews, to exit. We all followed the casket, walking almost as though we were trailing, parade-like behind the woman in the video.

♦ ♦ ♦

Years have passed since my late wife's funeral, and yet the power of this service will stay with my family and me until we follow her out that door in our own caskets.

---

2. John H. Sammis, "Trust and Obey" (1887). Public domain.
3. You can watch this video on YouTube at www.youtube.com/watch?v=OD nOTFgdTL8&t=2s.

Bobbie and I were married in 1970, almost forty-five years before this day. This wasn't the script I would have written. Or hoped for. But it was what it was.

So back to the Scripture verse that appeared on the screen after Bobbie's video. What are the "many seeds" produced from the death of that single seed falling to the ground and dying? It was Jesus who spoke these words just days prior to His own death on a cross. He was speaking to people who knew about seeds. Many made their living as farmers. They knew well that you can take seeds and put them in large pits or silos,[4] even in a decorative bowl on the table where you can admire them. But in order for seeds to do their work, they must be planted in the ground. When this happens, the chemicals in the earth strip the outer coating of the seed, giving the material inside a chance to grow into a plant, someday producing a harvest. And that harvest brings forth myriad more seeds.

Actually, the church on that day was filled with the yield of Bobbie's life. Her children, extended family, friends, neighbors, women in her Bible study, members of our church, and thousands watching by livestream. Bobbie's life was a bold testimony for Christ. As painful as it was for us, her death multiplied that witness around the world.

If Jesus—again the One who first spoke these words— had not died, we would not know Him. The power of His Holy Spirit would not be available to us. Our lives would not be what they are if the Kernel of Wheat hadn't fallen to the ground and died.

---

4. See "The History and Evolution of Grain Storage," LCDM, December 31, 2020, https://lcdmcorp.com/grain-flow-101/evolution-grain-storage.

The same is true of Bobbie's death. This is a hard reality. And a picture of God's redeeming grace.

BOBBIE KNEW

Two months before she died, Bobbie told two of her friends that she "hopes Robert marries Nancy Leigh DeMoss." But she didn't mention it to me. Honestly, I'm glad she didn't tell me. That might have felt like an assignment. But when I discovered this after Nancy and I were dating, it was a sweet confirmation.

Bobbie's and my "till death do us part" spoken at our wedding in 1970 provided a script for something brand-new forty-five years later.

Bobbie had met Nancy in 2003 when my literary agency represented her as an author. These two women discovered a shared love for God's Word and classic hymns. In spite of the geographic distance between them, their friendship became strong, full of mutual respect. Nancy watched the livestream of Bobbie's funeral in November 2014, even broadcasting an audio portion of it on her daily radio program, *Revive Our Hearts*.

The reason I'm talking about these things right here at the beginning of this book is that someday folks will be counting the "many seeds" . . . and the harvest . . . that will be produced when I "fall to the ground and die." At least I hope they will. You may be reading these words after that happens, and if you'd care to look into it, you may discover, by God's grace, some of those seeds. And the fruit. I'm truly trusting there's some good stuff.

This is both sobering and comforting for me. As it should be for you. So I have a question I'm hoping I have your permission to ask: When you die and your "kernel of wheat" falls to the ground and dies, what will your harvest look like? In this book, we're going to talk about that.

Many years ago, a good friend told me that a book is nothing if not a long letter from one person to another. Or an unhurried, one-on-one conversation seated across from each other at a small table in a coffee shop. My hope is that the adventure of reading this book will be like you and me having that conversation. Just us. It's that long letter, that extended conversation.

There are no platforms. No microphones or sound systems. There's only us . . . you and me. As I'm writing, I'm doing my best to lean in. To watch your face. To answer questions you may have as you read. To be clear. And honest. And kind.

At this point, since we're getting acquainted, it's important to me that you know I'm coming from the perspective of someone who is a Christ follower. And given the nature of the book's subject matter, I'm going to assume you're good with this. My hope is that if you're not, the pages that follow will draw you closer to knowing Jesus as your Savior. Nothing could be more important, especially as you approach the "finish line" of your life.

I have one overriding prayer as you begin reading—that our walking through these pages together will result in more wonderful yield from your "kernel of wheat" than there would have been without this experience. If that happens, our time will have been well worth it.

Welcome.

ROBERT WOLGEMUTH
Niles, Michigan

INTRODUCTION

BREAKING THE TAPE

The tape: a long, thin piece of material that is stretched across the finish line of a race to be broken by the first one across the line.

MERRIAM-WEBSTER

May the Lord keep you faithful in the race . . . all the way to the finish line.

NANCY DEMOSS WOLGEMUTH[1]

I t was the first time I had seen a dead body.

I must have been ten or eleven years old. My family had taken our annual pilgrimage to Winona Lake, Indiana, where my dad was attending Youth for Christ's annual

---

1. Nancy often concludes handwritten notes to friends with these words. She's been doing this for years.

conference. He was, for most of his adult life, an executive in this ministry.

The little town in North Central Indiana featured a world-famous conference center—which is why we were there—and a lake. It was here I learned to swim, though not by my own choosing.

Standing on the long pier that jutted out from the shore across the surface of the water, my oldest brother determined that this would be a good time to teach me to swim. Notice, I did not say, "to teach me *how* to swim." He simply pushed me into the water that was well over my head, figuring that the desperate moment of sheer terror would do all the necessary instructing. Thankfully—for my children, grandchildren, and great-grandson—he was right. Through the trauma of the event, and the gurgling and sputtering that ensued, I floated to the surface and swam.

Around that time, I witnessed an event at the lake that involved a married student who was attending Bethel Theological Seminary nearby. It was his last day on earth. What I remember was his panicked wife yelling for help from a pier not far from my swimming lesson and men dashing to the spot where he failed to surface and then pulling his body from the water a few minutes later. I ran to get a closer look.

This was before most people had heard of CPR or would have had any idea what those three letters meant. So they laid him faceup on the pier, and I stood there at a safe distance, gazing at his body. His wife was frantic, but no one was trying to revive him. We heard the sound of sirens headed our way. Straining to see everything, I looked at the graying frame of the twentysomething man who had just a few minutes before been like the rest of us at the lake that day, splashing around with his friends. I was close enough to see that his eyes were open. This sight haunted me for a long time.

Over the past sixty years or so, I've seen my share of corpses—mostly in funeral homes where the bodies have been properly outfitted, coiffed, and painted to camouflage the actual color and original shapes of their sunken faces.

Even though I have previously written about the moment that Bobbie, my wife of almost forty-five years, died,[2] I want to take a few minutes here to speak of it in more detail. In fact, it was this memory that inspired me to write the book you now hold.

My daughters, Missy and Julie, were sitting with me next to Bobbie's rented hospital bed plunked down in the middle of our living room in October 2014. Enid, our faithful hospice nurse, was also there. She had come by the house only fifteen or so minutes earlier. Enid had taken Bobbie's blood pressure. It was very low. She then tried to take Bobbie's pulse with her thumb on the backside of her wrist. At first, Enid told us it was faint. Then she told us there was none. Incredibly, we knew this because Bobbie had asked her.

"You don't feel a pulse, do you?" Bobbie queried.

"No, Miss Bobbie. I don't."

Bobbie asked for the head end of her hospital bed to be lowered so the whole thing would be flat. Then she reached out, took me by the shirt with both hands, drew my face

---

2. Robert Wolgemuth, *Like the Shepherd: Leading Your Marriage with Love and Grace* (Washington, DC: Salem, 2017).

within a couple inches of hers, and said, "I love you so much," as clearly as she had said it nearly five decades before when we fell in love. She closed her eyes and died.

"Is she dead?" Missy asked the nurse, her understandable panic not camouflaged.

"Yes," Enid said evenly after putting her hand on Bobbie's listless chest, holding it there for less than a minute. "She's not breathing."

Although there were plenty of tears later, my memory of this moment is that Missy, Julie, and I were too overwhelmed to do or say much at all. After thirty months of walking alongside this brave woman in her cancer journey, I can't say we were surprised by the inevitable. But the heaviness that smothered us when we realized Bobbie was gone is almost too sacred to try to describe.

I reached out to Bobbie's face and gently closed her eyelids.

Then I sat for a few minutes next to the hospital bed, watching as Bobbie's body slowly turned gray. Then cool to the touch.

Thirty minutes after my phone call to summon them, two body-bag-toting men from the funeral home arrived with a wheeled stretcher. My daughters and I stepped out of the living room while they slipped my wife's fragile form onto the stretcher. When they let us know they were ready, we joined them and what was once my vibrant wife in the foyer of our home. They had zipped up the bag, leaving only Bobbie's face visible. The men graciously stepped away.

Missy, Julie, and I took each other's hands and stood in a circle around the gurney carrying my late wife. Their late mother. We sang a song we had sung—oh, maybe a thousand times—when one of us was headed out of town or returning to college, or when a gathering at our house was breaking up. Bobbie had learned this song at River Valley Ranch in Manchester, Maryland, when she was a young girl: "Goodbye, our God is watching o'er you, Goodbye, His mercies go before you, Goodbye, and we'll be praying for you, So goodbye, may God bless you."[3]

When we finished singing, I offered a short "thank you" prayer for this woman's life and love and faith and beauty. I leaned over and softly kissed her cold forehead. Missy and Julie said their goodbyes. I nodded to the two men, who on that cue finished zipping the rubber cocoon over Bobbie's face and wheeled it out the front door to their van.

We have sung that song only once since that afternoon— almost two weeks later when our voices rang out as Bobbie's casket was being lowered into a yawning hole in the ground. But not since. It feels almost too holy to repeat under any other circumstances.

When we were married in 1970, Bobbie was just twenty years old, I was a much older twenty-two. Even though the "till death" phrase was part of our traditional wedding vows, it was the last thing on our minds.

For the ensuing four and a half decades, many times Bobbie told me she wanted to be "the first to die." I always demurred. Who wants to talk about death when the majority of your life stands before you? Not me.

But now I was facing the reality of Bobbie's wish. She

---

3. Wendell P. Loveless, "Goodbye" (Wheaton, IL: Hope Publishing, 1938).

was dead. I was a widower. Missy and Julie were launching the remainder of their young lives motherless.

Like so many around the globe each year, cancer was what captured her at sixty-four. The journey this disease took us on began with a visit to a woman's oncology clinic in 2012 at MD Anderson Cancer Center in Orlando, where we were living. When Bobbie, Julie, and I stepped off the elevator on the second floor, the waiting room was peppered with women. Some were reading a book, studying their smartphones, or quietly chatting with their husbands sitting close by. Others were alone, doing nothing. Almost all were bald. A few had their naked heads covered with a scarf or a knitted yarn beanie.

I wish I could adequately describe what I felt that day, but I cannot. The right words are beyond reach. That visit to the second floor marked the beginning of a thirty-month journey that ended that chilly October 2014 day when we sang the "Goodbye" song. Bobbie had been nothing short of a warrior. I tried to be too.

What I'd like to say right here at the beginning of a book about the end of life is that the experience of walking through death's door with my wife all but eliminated my fear of the same. Mostly, this was because of Bobbie's remarkable attitude about the inevitability of her demise after being diagnosed with Stage IV ovarian cancer.

Bobbie, with the certainty of her own death, showed me how to live without shaking her fist at the God in whom she trusted. In spite of what she actually went through, with me by her side, there was no complaining.

When I've told people that Bobbie didn't protest, even

during the horrendous effects of a chemotherapy followed by a clinical trial that literally made her feel like she was freezing to death, even in the heat of a Florida summer, their quizzical looks make clear they're wondering if I'm exaggerating. Even a little. I'm not. She did not whimper or complain, even hunched over the toilet throwing up the meager nutrition in her stomach. She'd finish vomiting. Struggle to her feet. And smile. Oh, and thank me for being there for her.

It's with the living example of my wife dying that I determined to embrace what I'll share with you in the pages that follow. With the historical perspective of the death of biblical patriarchs and some clues as to how you can prepare for your own death, I'm hoping the chapters that follow will encourage you and give you some specific ideas as you prepare for this day. I'm glad you've joined me on the adventure of writing a book about death. My death. Your death.

Thank you for the privilege of walking—or running . . . or crawling—through the contours of this. You and me.

Together to the finish line.

ONE

DEAD. NOT DEAD.

The original title of this, the opening chapter of a book on a serious subject was, "Yucky. Not Yucky." My editor wisely suggested something more grown-up-sounding. I'm good with adult words. However, having raised two daughters all the way from silliness to full maturity, clearly the word *yucky* was a favorite. The target of this word could have ranged from small sticky place on the kitchen counter to something much more serious. Like mortality.

The opening two chapters in the first book in the Bible paint a pristine picture of all things good. In some cases . . . *very* good. But when we arrive at chapter 3, the landscape changes. And everything in this Genesis chapter shows us what bad looks like. In some cases, *very* bad.

And one of those terrible things that resulted from Adam and Eve's disobedience was death. Until that moment, nothing or no one died. Then a decree went out that eventually everything would perish: "For you are dust, and you will return to dust" (Genesis 3:19 CSB).

Like, which part of this diagnosis don't we understand?

And the most sobering part of this God-spoken directive is that the word *you* isn't just delivered to Adam. The pronoun is plural. Thousands of years later, you and I are included. The people we have loved, the people we love now, and the people we will love tomorrow are in there. And the process of dying begins the moment we suck in our first big swallow of air as tiny newborns. Like an hourglass that's been flipped over, the sand above begins trickling below through the pinch in the middle. There's no turning that thing right side up. We're on a one-way trajectory.

And beyond the Garden of Eden and throughout the Bible and all of recorded history, there's plenty more that has been written about death.

For example, the man Job, from the depths of his own despair affirmed this to be true.

> Anyone born of woman
> is short of days and full of trouble.
> He blossoms like a flower, then withers;
> he flees like a shadow and does not last.
> (Job 14:1–2 CSB)

A flower that "does not last." A brilliant and descriptive metaphor for death.

Even the most beloved psalm written by David assumes life's end. He doesn't open this subject in the Shepherd's Psalm with "just in case" or "maybe"; rather he begins the death phrase with the conjunction "even though," like there's no choice in the matter. Because there isn't.

> Even though I walk
> through the darkest valley . . . (Psalm 23:4)

So because of the shortsightedness of Adam and Eve's disobedience, and the consequence, the Bible includes the stories of men and women dying. From these accounts you and I can learn a few important things. Here are some examples.

THE MURDER OF THE BIBLE'S SECOND SON

The verses immediately following the eating of the forbidden fruit tell of the birth of two boys—first Cain, then Abel.

Imagine the joy the parents of these men must have experienced at their births. And like every mother and dad throughout the remainder of recorded history with more than one child, Adam and Eve likely wondered, *How is it possible that these boys came from the same parents? They could not be more different from each other.*

If you're the parent of more than one kid, you've had this conversation with your mate, right?

Apparently, it was too much of a difference for Cain to bear.

"Cain said to his blow-dried, always-do-everything-right brother Abel, 'Let's go out to the field.' And while they were in the field, Cain attacked his brother Abel and killed him" (Genesis 4:8, Robert's paraphrase).

God's sentence of death directed to Adam's sinful decision struck first in his own family. It doesn't matter how long it was before Cain murdered his little brother, the sting must have been awful . . . for their dad and mom.

Remember that it had been many years since Adam and Eve had disobeyed God. We know this since there had been time for Cain and Abel to be conceived, born, and grow up. And don't you know that when their mother and father first learned of their son's murder, their minds must have careened back to God's declaration of the thing called death. And this, as a result of their own disobedience. Now death was paying a visit to their family. No small thing to be sure.

As you know, the whole idea of this book is that you and I are going to die. Someday we will cross that line. The event will be complete. The finish line will be our death.

It's a certainty.

Or is it?

A QUICK ROUND TRIP

When Jesus walked this earth, there were times when He went nose-to-nose with the Genesis 3 narrative about the sentence of death and literally brought departed people back to life. If this was the first time you've ever heard of this, what I just wrote would have sounded incredulous. Even impossible.

But you've likely heard there was a Man who lived and had the power to call dead people back. And according to the gospel accounts, Jesus did this three times. Just three times—not counting His own resurrection.

The first such miracle involved the only son of a widow. Take a second and let that sink in. Here was a lone woman who had lost her husband and her only child. Jesus and His disciples were visiting the town of Nain and happened upon a funeral procession. No one needed to tell Jesus about the circumstances. No one showed Him the press clipping that included the obituary. Jesus knew. Scripture says that Jesus saw the mother and had compassion on her and said, "Don't cry" (Luke 7:13).

Jesus approached the bier and did something no self-respecting Rabbi would ever do.[1] He touched the corpse and said, "Young man, I say to you, get up!" Immediately, "the dead man sat up and began to talk, and Jesus gave him back to his mother" (Luke 7:14–15).

The biblical account tells us that Jesus left the scene and got on to the next thing on His schedule. But can you imagine what the next few hours must have been like for the young man's mother? Dead son. Because of Jesus, not dead son.

The second account, found in Mark 5:21–43, is also a familiar one. This story has to do with a man named Jairus, the father of a daughter, which is probably why I'm so attracted to it.

---

1. "The prohibition of Kohen defilement to the dead is the commandment to a Jewish priest (*kohen*) not to come in direct contact with, or be in the same enclosed roofed space as a dead human body" (Wikipedia contributors, "Prohibition of Kohen Defilement by the Dead," *Wikipedia*, https://en.wikipedia.org/wiki/Prohibition_of _Kohen_defilement_by_the_dead, accessed August 10, 2022).

Another reason to love this story is the way Jairus, a decorated Jew, humbly fell at Jesus' feet, pleading on behalf of his twelve-year-old girl. For priests or Pharisees who may have been there, seeing a holy Israelite on the ground in front of an unschooled teacher like Jesus would have been scandalous. But Jairus didn't care what anyone thought. This was a nothing-to-lose split second.

Once Jesus arrived at the home of Mr. and Mrs. Jairus, He entered the youngster's room with her mother and father, Peter, James, and John. Given the likelihood of the size of the room, a crowded space, to be sure. And as He had done with the other dead body, Jesus broke protocol and took her hand. The tenderness of this scene overwhelms me. And like the man's corpse on the cart, the young girl immediately sat up. Dead daughter. Because of Jesus, not dead daughter.

And maybe the most famous Bible story of a dead person coming to life, doesn't include any touching at all. This time Jesus just spoke, as He had at the very beginning—at creation in Genesis—turning death into life.[2]

THE BETHANY CAPER

As you'll discover adventuring your way through the pages ahead, if there ever was a death-to-life head-scratcher, this is it.

First, a little backstory . . .

Jesus and His disciples were ministering in an area across

---

2. The Bible on Jesus and creation: John 1:3, 10; 1 Corinthians 8:6; Colossians 1:16; Hebrews 1:2.

the Jordan known as Bethabara. A messenger arrived with the news that their friend Lazarus, Mary and Martha's brother, was sick. Deathly sick. The three lived in Bethany, a full fifteen to twenty miles away from where Jesus was. Without the availability of high-tech communication, there was no way to let Jesus know about His friend immediately. Instead, it likely took the courier a full day to deliver the news.

That means by the time Jesus heard the news, Lazarus was likely already dead. And I believe the next forty-eight hours proves it. And Jesus—being God also—knew.

Think about it. The messenger arrived in Jesus' presence, doubled over in exhaustion, his sides aching. His twenty-mile run—just six miles short of a marathon—had wiped him out. He made this journey as a gift to Mary and Martha, Jesus' dear friends. And through heaves and gasps, the runner told the Savior that His buddy Lazarus was sick. Really sick.

Jesus' blink response sounds rude. Really rude. "This sickness will not end in death" (John 11:4).

I'm more than a little scandalized just thinking about how this must have sounded. It's as though Jesus, having received the news, yawned.

Was He being discourteous? Did He make a mistake by not dropping everything and hurrying to Bethany? Was this an oversight? A blip on an ordinarily seamlessly planned itinerary? Or was this a perfect scenario for a message His friends would have never embraced if Lazarus hadn't caught this terminal disease? And died. In fact, might this just be a perfect place setting for a dinner party that will feed the world?

Lazarus is dead. Then he's not dead.

So watch this. Carefully. Then decide for yourself.

Lazarus, a resident of the little settlement of Bethany, contracts a deadly virus. Or gets sick another way. He may have fallen off a stepladder . . . more about that in a minute. We aren't told. His sisters Mary and Martha summon the fastest runner in town and beg him to find Jesus. Somehow this guy hears that the Teacher is in a town some twenty miles away. He turns and runs as fast as he can on the shortest route, due north.

Since the terrain features rocks and potholes and hills, nothing like a track or a paved roadway, it takes him a day to arrive. Before the volunteer is able to deliver his message, Lazarus dies. Not having any idea that this grueling race is a waste of his time, the courier tells Jesus that Mary and Martha's brother is sick.

Knowing that Lazarus had already breathed his last, Jesus' response upon receiving the message from the fatigued athlete is more than curious. Jesus said, "This sickness will not end in death. No, it is for God's glory so that God's Son may be glorified through it" (John 11:4).

Let me paint the picture: The ancient equivalent to Jim Ryun runs twenty miles; he's now in Jesus' presence, leaning forward with his hands on his knees; "Jim" gasps out his assigned dispatch and tells Jesus that His friend is about to die. Jesus smacks him down and argues with the message. "Lazarus is *not* dying; I'll go and see for myself. In two days, God's glory is about to be revealed. And here's the kicker: the glory will be unwrapped by way of Me."

If you and I were to be able to watch a YouTube video of this exchange, we'd see that there was no marching band. No fanfare or confetti. No platform, bright lights, worship

bands, or microphones. But this is one of the most consequential moments in the history of the world. What Jesus
says in the face of what should have been tragic news became
the most important newsflash. Ever. It's my reason for taking
a few hours to sit with you and talk about death.

I'll get back to the narrative in a minute, but let me jump
ahead and give you the punch line:

You and I are going to die; it's for sure. Today we don't
know how. We only know the "that."

As you read these words, the fact of your eventual death
may be highly disturbing. I get that. In fact, I've always lived
with a sense of caution—fear of dying—in nearly everything I do. You may be different, throwing yourself into life,
tossing discretion to the wind. Skydiving, rock climbing,
high-speed motorcycles may be a part of the fabric of your
world. That's good. Not me.

My besetting fear is heights . . . *acrophobia*.

Since in so many cases falling equals dying, what if
instead of anxiety about heights, my paralyzing phobia was
death? What if the thought of dying freaked me out? Not
surprisingly, there's a name for this too: *thanatophobia*.

Google this word, and you'll get a boatload of articles
about this debilitating fear.

So one way or another, you and I are going to die.

However, and stay with me here, you and I are *not* going
to die—that's also for sure.

In other words, if we put our faith in Jesus Christ and
embrace the good news of the gospel for ourselves before this
inevitable death, we will live forever. That's God's promise.

Got it? Good.

Confused? Let me explain.

This story may sound like a simple, familiar scenario. A man named Lazarus gets sick. Man dies. Jesus tries to come to the rescue but too late. I thought this was the world's greatest Friend. The Savior. The One who always answers. That's true, but people die every day. In spite of the prayers of friends and family, they die. Funerals are held and people say nice things about the departed, including the belief that Jesus still cares.

> YOU AND I ARE *NOT* GOING TO DIE. IN OTHER WORDS, IF WE PUT OUR FAITH IN JESUS CHRIST AND EMBRACE THE GOOD NEWS OF THE GOSPEL FOR OURSELVES BEFORE THIS INEVITABLE DEATH, WE WILL LIVE FOREVER. THAT'S GOD'S PROMISE.

So did Lazarus die so people would learn a lesson about "the brevity of life" and "the inevitability of death"? Or was there a larger mission?

Jesus had the power to turn ordinary water into fine wine. To feed thousands. To drive out demons. To heal the sick. But I guess with Lazarus, not this time: "Now Jesus loved Martha and her sister and Lazarus. So when he heard that Lazarus was sick, he stayed where he was two more days" (John 11:5–6).

Wait. What?

Jesus received the desperate news about this friend and decided to do . . . nothing. For two days.

This is more than curious. In fact, to add to the weirdness, Thomas, the disciple not known among his colleagues as Mr. Positivity, predictably reminds Jesus that the last time He was near this town, the loudmouths tried to stone Him.

Instead of giving him a straight answer, Jesus' response to Thomas feels like what it would be like to have your car break down on a lonely country road and AAA ends up sending a theologian instead of a mechanic. Not exactly what Thomas was hoping for.[3]

Jesus hears that Lazarus is really sick. But instead of hiking up His robe and hurrying over to Bethany to help, Jesus talks about daylight and stumbling in the night. Here's exactly what He said: "Are there not twelve hours of daylight? Anyone who walks in the daytime will not stumble, for they see by this world's light. It is when a person walks at night that they stumble, for they have no light" (John 11:9–10).

To add to the confusion about what He said, once Jesus had been faced with the opportunity to do something about His terminal friend, He *immediately* waits for forty-eight hours. When confronted with a real crisis, He speaks what sounded like a non sequitur, waxing theoretical. Or at least that may be what His disciples concluded in that moment.

Can you picture the quizzical look on these men's faces? Is the same perplexing look on your face as you read this? Me too.

However, Jesus was up to something. He always is.

Go back to verse 5 in our story. It reminds us that Jesus loved Mary and Martha. And He goes about proving it by letting their brother die. Seriously? Yes. For if Lazarus hadn't perished, the lesson would not have been taught. Or believed.

As we've seen from the exchange in the Garden of Eden, death became the certain penalty for sin. It was the result of

---

3. This helpful analogy is not mine. It belongs to Alistair Begg.

choosing darkness instead of light. God's punishment for the first couple was turning the lights off. That's the bad news. But the good news is that without the night, there's no joy in the sunrise. You don't even notice a burning candle in the daylight. But at night, that flaming candle can keep you from brushing your teeth with antiseptic cream instead of toothpaste or falling down the stairs. The light that shines in the pitch-darkness shows you where you are. And who you are. It changes everything. When Jesus referred to Himself as the Light of the world, this is what He was talking about.

THE TALK WITH MARTHA

Fast-forward a couple days. Jesus waits His forty-eight hours and then makes the one-day journey to Bethany.

The Lazarus odyssey lasts exactly four days. Right before Lazarus dies, a runner volunteers to go tell Jesus that he's sick. This hasty hike takes *a day*. Jesus gets the message and waits for *two days*. There's *three*. Then He walks back to Bethany to see these things for Himself. That's another day, which brings us to *four days*.

What I'd love is for you and me to carefully review the conversation Jesus had with Martha when He arrived in Bethany.

The news that Jesus is in the neighborhood—maybe by way of another fast runner—reaches their home, and it's Martha who comes out. Scripture says that Mary stays inside. Maybe too grief-stricken about her brother's death. Sullen and maybe even angry that Jesus hasn't come to their rescue.

I guess it's not strange that instead of falling apart emotionally, Martha cuts to the chase: "'Lord,' Martha said to Jesus, 'if you had been here, my brother would not have died'" (John 11:21).

Fair thing to say.

This is where the focus tightens on the "light and dark" thing Jesus mentioned to His disciples back in Bethabara. In fact, it's the reason for—and the message of—this book. Death is the promise. It's the reality of darkness that makes light that much sweeter.

It's the very reason Jesus said to His disciples, "Lazarus is dead, and for your sake I am glad I was not there, so that you may believe" (John 11:14–15).

> THE CERTAINTY OF OUR DEATH FORCES US TO LOOK MORE CAREFULLY AT OUR LIVES.

The certainty of our death forces us to look more carefully at our lives. If I didn't know that death would bring me face-to-face with a holy God who will judge me appropriately, I might not be as eager to prepare.

WHAT'S SO GREAT ABOUT JESUS?

Go with me to the chat between Jesus and Martha. Lazarus has expired, hanging out in a tomb for four days. Martha is understandably grieving. And maybe a little upset that Jesus, who could have done something to help her ailing brother, doesn't seem as troubled. In fact, He hasn't even bothered to come to be with her and Mary.

Then Jesus says to her evenly, "Your brother will rise again" (John 11:23).

Martha is confused, wondering about the actual timing of her brother's resurrection. But for the moment, this doesn't matter. What she cares about is that she misses her sibling and wants him back now. But in that moment Jesus did what He had done two days ago when He first heard about Lazarus's failing health. He did nothing.

> YOU HAVE NOT WASTED YOUR LIFE—YOUR TRAGEDIES, YOUR TRIUMPHS, YOUR FAILURES, YOUR JOYS. YOU CAN TRUST JESUS.

As you know, in 2014, I buried my wife. The sound you could hear as her casket was being lowered into the ground was the gruesome tearing of flesh. Mine. And my daughters and grandkids. Extended family and many dear friends standing close by. There was more pain than you could know.

From the time I was a small boy, I heard people telling other people in my situation with a very sick loved one to "just rest in Jesus." Or "trust Jesus." Or "lean on Jesus." The day after Bobbie's burial, I went back to the cemetery. There was a mountain of freshly cut flowers, now beginning to wither and die, piled up on the spot.

"So what are you going to do now, Robert?" I actually heard myself saying quietly. The recording in my head replayed what I have said a thousand times in my lifetime and heard plenty of times since Bobbie got sick. "Take it to Jesus."

If I were to slip on the hat of a cynical man, I could ask the question you see above: "What's so great about Jesus?"

I've spent a lifetime teaching the Bible and having the

privilege of authoring a bunch of books that tell the gospel story one way or another. My dream early this morning and the past few hours as I pounded away on my keyboard with these words was to be able to ask this question: "What's so great about Jesus?"

And here's the answer:

Not long after the hard conversation with Martha, Jesus said to His disciples something about the reason there really is something "so great" about Him.

"My Father's house has many rooms; if that were not so, would I have told you that I am going there to prepare a place for you?" (John 14:2)

In other words, once you've finished your life, once you've pounded out the words of your story on your laptop, and are ready to cross over, you can rest easy. You have not wasted your life—your tragedies, your triumphs, your failures, your joys. You can trust Jesus.

He will be there. His promises are sure. You can count on Him. Between now and then, He can keep writing your story regardless of how many years you have.

A PRETEND VISIT WITH MARY, MARTHA, LAZARUS . . . YOU AND ME

The story of Lazarus's death was toward the end of Jesus' earthly ministry. That means that it wasn't long until He went to the cross and died, was buried, and then rose from the grave.

Let's pretend that after Jesus reappeared to His disciples and visibly ascended to Heaven, you and I make a lunch appointment with Mary, Martha, and Lazarus. It's just the five of us.

In this setting, we're able to ask about the time when Lazarus got really sick. We ask Mary and Martha what it was like to have to wait four days before their friend Jesus showed up to help them. We may even have some fun asking Lazarus about the experience of being dead—if he remembers—and what that was like.

Our favorite part may be asking Lazarus how it felt to wake up to the sound of Jesus' voice and his name to "come out," struggling to stand to his feet and then step into the sunlight, and what freedom felt like when his friends obeyed Jesus and unwrapped the grave clothes so he could walk free.

But my most important question would be aimed at Martha. I would ask her to recall the one-on-one when Jesus finally came walking up to their house. Lazarus was still in the grave and questions came pouring out of her mouth . . . and her broken soul.

I would ask Martha to tell me what she thought when Jesus said to her: "I am the resurrection and the life. The one who believes in me will live, even though they die; and whoever lives by believing in me will never die. Do you believe this?" (John 11:25–26).

What a question Jesus asks. Do we believe, in the way Jesus told Martha, that you and I will never die? Do I?

The events of the past several weeks had been filled with anxiety for Martha and Mary . . . and Lazarus. With questions of life. And healing. And death. Yucky death.

As we're preparing to finish our lunch together, someone, I'm not sure who, makes a statement we won't ever forget. It's what I'd like to say to you, my reading friend, right here at the beginning of our conversation.

You are going to die. I am going to die. Unlike Lazarus, our visit to our graves will not be four days long.

But if Jesus is your Savior, if you invite Him to be there at your tomb, your death will last a lot shorter than four days. Your corpse is going into the ground to await the resurrection. Your soul/spirit is going immediately into the Lord's presence.

I'm remembering something I read a long time ago. It's a quote from the simple shoe and boot salesman turned bold preacher Dwight L. Moody:

Someday you will read in the papers that D. L. Moody of East Northfield, is dead. Don't you believe a word of it! At that moment I shall be more alive than I am now.[4]

You and I are going to die.
You and I are not going to die.
You get this now, don't you?

4. William R. Moody, *The Life of Dwight L. Moody* (New York: Revell, 1900), 554–55.

TWO

SPOILER ALERT . . . HEAVEN CAN BE YOURS

*Our views of the afterlife often make God an after-
thought. We imagine reunions with loved ones, no
disease, no pain, no sin, no suffering, no tears—all
gloriously true! But Heaven is Heaven because God
is there.*

DR. LUKE STAMPS, TWEET,
FEBRUARY 13, 2022

Even though the title of this book connotes a physical activity, a race with beginning and an end, you and I know that we're a lot more tired at the end than we were at the start. Given the rigors of his work and the persecution he endured, the apostle Paul knew something about this. And so

26

he wrote about a physical place that will house a resting place for those who know Christ as Savior. A forever dwelling.

"For we know," wrote Paul, "that if the earthly tent we live in is destroyed, we have a building from God, an eternal house in heaven, not built by human hands" (2 Corinthians 5:1).

Heaven is a place. A specific, someday visible reality. In the last chapter, I quoted Jesus' promise to His disciples about the mansions He was preparing for them. In Heaven: "My Father's house has many rooms; if that were not so, would I have told you that I am going there to prepare a place for you?" (John 14:2).

My favorite feature of Jesus' statement is the double down of His message. First, Heaven is better than those mansions you and I see when our computers invite us to "visit" some famous person's home.[1] Or just like in those home make-over shows where we watch the faces of the unsuspecting recipients of the complete refurbishing of their ordinary places into spectacular ones, Heaven's mansion is glorious. Amazing.

Second, Jesus sort of tweaks them with His follow-up. "If that were not so . . ." It was like He was saying, "Hey, guys. If this weren't true, why would I have gone to the effort to tell you about it?"

Don't you just love that?

Earthly death is real. From the experience of losing people we have loved, you and I know it. And so, according

---

1. I have been tempted to check these out. Along with their private jets and amazing cars. I've even succumbed to this nudge.

to the creation account and God's only Son's affirmation, is Heaven. Perhaps nothing alerts us to the reality of this more poignantly than an actual first-person account from a friend.

The woman who wrote the following is a close friend of my wife, Nancy. The account is about this friend's dad, Del Fehsenfeld, Jr.:

January 7 at 11:55 p.m. my father was escorted to Heaven. What a beautiful illustration God gave us of how exciting it is to be there. Dad's eyes got so big all of a sudden. He had tears in his eyes that trickled down his face; he began to show excitement. His mouth moved, and then there was a smile. He was trying to talk and say something. That was the most movement we had seen in days. Within the last thirty minutes, he had numerous times showed excitement and peace. The last time, though, was the most dramatic. It was so obvious he was being escorted to Heaven.

Mary, my sister, and I were able to sing songs and talk to him during this time. What a peace was on his face as God took him to Heaven. We are so grateful that God allowed us to see his entrance to Heaven. I told a nurse standing nearby, "This is the day he has lived for all his life."

You have read—maybe have seen or experienced—accounts like this. People who knew the wonder of God's grace in their own lives, standing on the threshold of eternity, seeing Heaven for themselves. It's quite amazing, isn't it?

Crossing the finish line is going to be a celebration like

you cannot imagine. Even better. It's Christmas morning when you were a kid. It's your honeymoon. It's the birth of your first child. Or grandchild. Or great-grandchild. It's your favorite team winning the championship. The word is way overused, but this time it fits: one day your finish line is going to be *awesome*.

Perhaps no Christian writer and thinker has done more to help us grasp something of the wonder of Heaven than Randy Alcorn. First published in 2004, Alcorn's book titled *Heaven* has sold way more than a million copies.[2] He writes, "If you're a child of God, you do not just 'go around once' on Earth. You don't get just one earthly life. You get another— one far better and without end. You'll inhabit the New Earth! You'll live with the God you cherish and the people you love as an undying person on an undying Earth."[3]

Another Christian "expert" on longing for Heaven is our precious friend Joni Eareckson Tada. In her own book, *Heaven: Your Real Home*, she writes, "Every Christian who keeps looking up stretches his or her heart's capacity for heaven."[4]

> CROSSING THE FINISH LINE IS GOING TO BE A CELEBRATION LIKE YOU CANNOT IMAGINE. IT'S CHRISTMAS MORNING WHEN YOU WERE A KID. IT'S YOUR HONEYMOON. IT'S THE BIRTH OF YOUR FIRST CHILD.

---

2. Randy C. Alcorn, *Heaven* (Carol Stream, IL: Tyndale, 2004). You see this once in a while. "Sold a million copies." If the claims are true, this is a big deal. Thin air for a book. The average book sells around five thousand copies.

3. Alcorn, *Heaven*, 415.

4. Joni Eareckson Tada, *Heaven: Your Real Home* (1995; repr., Grand Rapids, Zondervan, 2018), 280.

And with the sound of wonder in her voice and twinkle in her eye, we can hear and see her say this:

> If God brings our pets back to life, it wouldn't surprise me. It would be just like Him. It would be totally in keeping with His generous character . . . Exorbitant. Excessive. Extravagant in grace after grace. Of all the dazzling discoveries and ecstatic pleasures heaven will hold for us, the potential of seeing Scrappy would be pure whimsy—utterly joyfully, surprisingly superfluous . . . Heaven is going to be a place that would refract and reflect in as many ways as possible the goodness and joy of our great God, who delights in lavishing love on His children.[5]

When people like Randy Alcorn and Joni Eareckson Tada, contemporary writers and wise thinkers, go on and on about the wonder and reality of Heaven, it should convince us, then make us like ebullient kids on their birthdays.

Centuries ago, the apostle Paul also weighed in on this issue about death and Heaven. First, the promise of glory gave him perspective on life when he wrote at the beginning of his letter to the folks living in Philippi: "For to me, to live is Christ and to die is gain" (Philippians 1:21).

Later in the same letter, Paul penned, "Brothers and sisters, I do not consider myself yet to have taken hold of it. But one thing I do: Forgetting what is behind and straining toward what is ahead, I press on toward the goal to win

5. Joni Eareckson Tada, *Holiness in Hidden Places* (Nashville: Countryman, 1999), 133.

the prize for which God has called me heavenward in Christ Jesus . . . Our citizenship is in heaven" (3:13–14, 20).

The night before Bobbie died, our daughters, Missy and Julie, were with her as she rested on the rented hospital bed in the living room. After several weeks of caring for my wife, I had slipped off to bed. As her primary caregiver for months, I was more exhausted than I ever remembered being. I wasn't there when she repeated over and over again, "Be still, and know that I am God" (Psalm 46:10), each time emphasizing a different word. She also reported to our daughters that she "saw children playing and white twinkle lights."

It must have really been something special for her. Like it will be for you and me. So wonderful. Even better than the metaphorical experience of this man . . .

You may have heard of a guy named Rick Hansen. Back in 1987, few people in North America didn't know about him. His name and the wonder of his story were invoked in coffee shops, church narthexes, and barber shops everywhere.[6]

But just in case you haven't heard of him or just aren't remembering who he is, let me stroke the refresh key.

Born in 1957, a scrappy, athletic fifteen-year-old Canadian named Richard Marvin (Rick) Hansen was returning home from a fishing trip with his buddies. He made the unforced teen error of riding in the open bed of a pickup truck with his friend Dan Alder. The driver lost control of the vehicle and slammed into a tree, launching the boys, first in the air, then violently into a ditch. Alder emerged uninjured. Hansen was not as fortunate, crashing to the earth on

6. "Rick Hansen," *The Canadian Encyclopedia*, March 24, 2008; last modified March 21, 2019, www.thecanadianencyclopedia.ca/en/article/rick-hansen.

his head. The impact severed his spinal cord, rendering him a lifetime paraplegic.

Facing the specter of life in a wheelchair, the young man could have yanked the plug on the years he had left, consigning himself to a pathetic existence as an invalid. However, the span of Rick's life became a travelogue of remarkable achievements, the pinnacle showcasing his "Man in Motion World Tour."

On March 21, 1985, strapped in his wheelchair, his useless legs tucked tightly in front of him, Rick began what would be a twenty-six-month trek of nearly 25,000 miles, the equivalent of circling the globe, raising funds for spinal cord research. The grueling trip took him through thirty-four countries on four continents. On the way, he faced all kinds of extreme weather—heat, rain, blizzards, windstorms. Rick made his way across all kinds of terrain—deserts, forests, mountains. Mile after mile, he persevered, inflicting incredible wear and tear on his weary body.

Finally, the journey's summit happened on May 22, 1987, at Vancouver's BC Place in front of more than fifty thousand people. The celebration included dignitaries of every conceivable stripe. Complete strangers gleefully double high-fived each other. Typically somber and stoic Canadians wept at the sight.

After completing what's hard to even imagine with our mortal senses, Rick glided across the finish line he had invested more than two years of his life to successfully traverse. A finish line for the record books to be sure.

◆ ◆ ◆

Death was not part of God's original plan for mankind. It's true. The exquisite Garden of Eden was, in fact, all the Heaven our first parents should have needed.

When Adam and Eve were created, they were placed in a perfect place. A lush and beautiful garden. Their fellowship with every living thing, including God and each other, was unspoiled.

Dreadfully, when the serpent proffered a lie to the unsuspecting Eve, she caved. Here's the record of their awful conversation:

> The woman said to the serpent, "We may eat the fruit from the trees in the garden. But about the fruit of the tree in the middle of the garden, God said, 'You must not eat it or touch it, or you will die.'"
>
> "No! You will certainly not die," the serpent said to the woman. (Genesis 3:2–4 CSB)

So she reached out and grasped the forbidden fruit, took a bite, and offered it to her husband. He shamelessly surrendered, doing the same. The consequence was inevitable and terrible and historic. In fact, centuries later, the writer of the book of Hebrews included a sentence that would not have been necessary had the garden conversation turned out differently: "It is appointed for people to die once—and after this, judgment . . ." (Hebrews 9:27 CSB).

This biblical text cannot be denied. It leaves no doubt. Someday we will stop breathing. Our heart will squeeze for the last time. Our warm, soft skin will be exchanged for a cold, tawny replacement. Our eyes will slowly deflate and recede in their sockets; our mouths will dry up, never to move or make a sound again. You and I will be dead.

The certainty of my own death has taken residence in my thinking from the time I was a small boy. This may sound unusually morose, but it's true. Maybe it's because every time I went to church in Lancaster County with my grandparents or cousins, a graveyard was visible and accessible. Right there beside the church, next to the parking lot. At times, I'd detour long enough to look at the granite markers. The ones chiseled with "Wolgemuth" or "Dourte" (my mother's maiden name) magnetically drew me. Death seemed ever so present.

The relatives we were visiting in Pennsylvania were mostly farmers. Dying was an integral part of their lives. This book is about crossing the finish line. Death. Both you and me. And although reading this could feel like your first steps on a grim journey, I would love for you to picture Rick Hansen's return to his blessed Canadian homeland after a challenging—sometimes gruesome—trip. Bathed in a cacophony of earsplitting cheers, the man glided his wheelchair home.

Your finish line—whenever you cross it—can be such a spine-tingling celebration. My sole ambition in writing this is to assure you of exactly that.

◆ ◆ ◆

When I began crafting this manuscript, the thought washed over me that this may be the last book I write. My journey will be reaching its destination. Then it dawned on me that, regardless of your age, it may be the last book you read. Both of these are sobering things to consider, aren't they?

Of course, I don't know that I'll not write another book or that you'll not read another book, but given my age and the uncertainties of life you and I face each day, both are possible. And if this is true, what does it mean and how should we feel about it?

When my daughters were small, I sometimes took them to a shopping mall close to our home. I was looking for a way to give their mom a little break. They were anticipating an adventure. On one visit to this eclectic assortment of stores, I remember their becoming tired of what felt to them like aimless wandering. Their feet were dragging. But soon they realized I wasn't rambling. I was headed to a particular store. The ice cream and candy store. Once they knew where we were going, everything changed. Instead of coaxing them along, they were dragging me to the destination and could hardly wait to get there. If we know Christ as our Savior, Heaven, our ultimate destination, magnetically draws us to the finish line.

So if this is true, if we really do have something to look forward to, the fear we usually feel about the whole idea of death should dissipate . . . if not disappear.

As I read the books I gathered for groundwork for this one, yellow highlighter in hand, I began collecting wisdom from strangers who had taken the time to research and write important stuff about death. Since beginning this process, I've actually become acquainted with a few of the writers. But mostly, except for the fact that I soaked in the goodness of their hard work, they remain shadow acquaintances.

One of these "friends" is—or, should I say, was—Rob Moll, a brilliant writer. Rob's first book, *The Art of Dying*, was extremely helpful.[7] Even though we had never met, our lives crossed with mutual acquaintances in Chicago's northwest suburbs. I don't need to do any research on this, but his time at Christianity Today, his work with World Vision, and even his undergraduate studies at Cedarville University seal the fact that we knew some of the same folks.

Tragically, in July 2019, Rob slipped and fell to his death as he was hiking at Mount Rainier. He was forty-one years old. The excellent book Rob wrote was about death. He surely couldn't have had any idea that his book would be read so soon after his own demise.

Rob's good friend and colleague Ted Olsen wrote a touching article about him the week after Rob's accident:

> It's one interest of his I've been thinking a lot about this week. For years, Rob thought a lot about death. He volunteered as a hospice chaplain and took a part-time job at a funeral home even before he decided to write his first book, *The Art of Dying*. Why, I wondered, was such a young guy so interested in learning how to die well? Isn't that something to think about after midlife? Few healthy and athletic 41-year-olds are as prepared for their death as Rob was. Few are so aware of their own mortality, their short time on earth, and the opportunity to seize our brief moment here with joy, curiosity, and rich relationships.
>
> I am in deep grief over Rob's death. Other than my

---

7. Rob Moll, *The Art of Dying: Living Fully into the Life to Come* (Downers Grove, IL: InterVarsity, 2010).

wife, the person I'd most like to talk to about it is Rob himself. He'd have some wise things to say.[8]

"We all need to learn to die well, whatever age we are," is one of Rob's most poignant quotes.[9] Given the brevity of his own life, this statement is dramatically even more powerful. And here's another from Rob: "It is good to look death in the eye and constantly remind ourselves that our hope is in God, who defeated death."[10]

> "WE ALL NEED TO LEARN TO DIE WELL, WHATEVER AGE WE ARE."

The book in your hand right now is about death. But the last two words from Rob Moll—"defeated death," a concept found in Scripture[11]—remind us that although death is a formidable enemy, like death itself, it's dead.

And the reward for those who are "in Christ" is this: Heaven is waiting. For you and me. It's going to be more wonderful than we can imagine.

CROSSING HOME PLATE

The baseball equivalent to the finish line in track would be stepping on home plate after a home run. Especially a historic, bases-clearing round-tripper.

---

8. Ted Olsen, "Remembering Rob Moll," *Christianity Today*, July 26, 2019, www.christianitytoday.com/ct/2019/july-web-only/remembering-rob-moll.html.

9. Moll, *Art of Dying*, 157.

10. Moll, *Art of Dying*, 26.

11. See 1 Corinthians 15:55–57.

At this point, I'm happy to let you know that I've been a lifelong Chicago Cubs fan. In fact, after marrying Nancy in late 2015, it didn't take long for me to fill her in on my affection for the game generally and the Windy City northsiders specifically. When the season began in the spring of 2016, Nancy discovered a 106-year World Series victory drought that was the story of this professional baseball team. Six months later, in game seven of the World Series, the Cubs defeated the vaunted Cleveland Indians in what may have been the most emotional win in series history. At least it was for me.

If Nancy was an amateur enthusiast in 2016, her status changed to seasoned veteran in the years to come. Often, when I go to sleep at night, Nancy, sitting next to me in our bed, has the Cubs app open on her cell phone. Games against West Coast teams generally have barely started by the time I'm out for the night. But my lady somehow manages to keep her eye on the box score as she works on other projects on her laptop.

On August 13, 2018, almost two years after the Cubs hosted a parade in Chicago that boasted five million people in person, the seventh largest gathering in world history,[12] Nancy was still listening to the games as often as she could.

On this day, the Cubs were up against the Washington Nationals. It was a night game at Wrigley Field, something I never experienced as a kid since the Cubs didn't install lights

---

12. Joey Gelman, "Cubs World Series Celebration Ranks as 7th Largest Gathering in Human History," WGN Radio, November 5, 2016, https://wgnradio .com/dave-plier/cubs-worlds-series-celebration-ranks-as-7th-largest-gathering-in -human-history.

until 1988. The thing that made this moment in 2018 special was that every youngster pretending to be a major leaguer says the following out loud, even though completely alone in the backyard where no one can hear.

> Home team down three runs. Bases loaded, bottom of the ninth, two strikes on the batter, a rookie off the bench as a pinch hitter. The pitcher rocks and fires. The batter swings with all his might. A fly ball. Is it deep enough? This ball's got a chaaaannce. Gone![13]

This is precisely what happened that night. Every detail.

David Bote was a twenty-five-year-old rookie, having played for the Myrtle Beach Pelicans in 2016 and the South Bend Cubs in 2017, and then because of a vacancy on the roster, he graduated to the bigs in 2018. On this historic day, Joe Maddon, the Cubs skipper, called on the rookie to salvage an unlikely win after 8 and 2/3 innings of shutout baseball at the hands of Nationals ace Max Scherzer.

The next morning, Steven Green, the Cubs official photographer, posted a picture on Instagram that showed David Bote rounding third base, headed for home and a bombastic, if not dangerous, welcome. Like who decided that the best way to show a teammate that you're proud of him is to toss him back and forth and then rip off his jersey?

If you could see the photo of David Bote coming around third base, you'd see his outstretched arms, making him appear to be flying. And if you could see the look on the

---

13. This last sentence is exactly what Chicago Cubs radio announcer Pat Hughes says.

faces of his teammates who were surrounding home plate—their body language needs no explanation. They could not wait to welcome their young teammate. And the look on the faces of the loyal Cubs fans, who had just witnessed something they'd never forget, says all that needs to be said.

I first saw the photo the next morning after the jubilation at Wrigley. The person who posted it on Instagram used a single, simple word as a caption.[14]

Whether breaking the tape at the end of the final straightaway or wheeling into a stadium after 25,000 miles in a wheelchair or touching home plate after a walk-off, it's all that needed to be said:

Heaven

♦   ♦   ♦

My friend Tim Challies knows a thing or two about the subject, having suddenly lost his twenty-one-year-old son in early November 2020. Tim said it this way:

> And so, if heaven is, indeed real, and if the gateway that leads from this life really does open into the next, wouldn't it make sense that we enter with a cry of victory, a shout of triumph, a declaration of vindication? Wouldn't it make sense that our first thought is one of jubilation, that our first action is one of celebration, that our first sense is one of the truest and best kind of relief?

---

14. If you google "david bote grand slam photo," you'll see the amazing picture of the rookie baseball player flying home.

Wouldn't it make sense that when we have fought the good fight and finished the race and kept the faith, that we cross a kind of finish line and celebrate like an athlete? For in that moment we will know—we will know beyond all speculation, beyond all doubting, beyond all need for faith—that every effort was worth it, that no moment of suffering was in vain, that no sorrow will go uncomforted, that no ache will go unsoothed, that no tear will be left undried.[15]

Don't you just love that?

Tim also wrote:

We will know that though we dropped our anchor into the depths of an ocean whose bottom we could not see, it fastened securely to the rock. We will know that though we walked and limped and stumbled toward a city whose gates were obscured from our view, they opened to receive us. We will know that though we fought our way toward a destination we could see only with the eyes of faith, our faith was well-placed. "I knew it!" we will shout in triumph. "I knew it was real! I knew he was true!" we will cry, as we fall into the arms of the Savior.[16]

So there you have it. As Joni said, Heaven is "your real home." It's a spoiler alert that doesn't really spoil anything.

---

15. Tim Challies, "I Knew It!" @*Challies* (blog), November 29, 2021, www .challies.com/articles/i-knew-it. Used with permission. Tim also writes about this in his book *Seasons of Sorrow: The Pain of Loss and the Comfort of God* (Grand Rapids: Zondervan, 2022), which I highly recommend.
16. Challies, "I Knew It!"

THREE

FINISH LINE LINES

If you want to change the world, pick up your pen and write.

MARTIN LUTHER

N ice finish."

My brother-in-law—and dear friend—was walking through my garage. He passed the little red, freshly detailed, fifteen-year-old, four-cylinder two-seater convertible I had bought for Nancy on her birthday a few years before. Really good at noticing this kind of thing, Stan remarked, "There must be clear coat on your car."[1]

He gently stroked the fender with the back of his hand and added these words: "Nice finish."

---

1. Clear coat car paint is paint or resin with no pigments and hence imparts no color to the car. It's simply a layer of clear resin applied over colored coats. Almost 95 percent of all vehicles manufactured today have a clear coat finish.

Of course, I thanked him. What man doesn't appreciate it when another man—also a car guy—he respects compliments him on his car? In this case, the word *finish* had nothing to do with the title of this book. As you may remember, assuming you didn't doze through English class when this was explained, words that are spelled the same but have more than one meaning are called "homonyms."

Homonyms. Does this word ring a memory bell? In this book, we're talking about the kind of finish that completes the race rather than the sheen on your fender.

Okay, I'm done, but back to it in a few pages.

Class dismissed.

FAMOUS LAST WORDS . . . SPOKEN WHEN PEOPLE CROSSED THEIR FINISH LINES

Because of the proliferation of end-of-life care in hospitals and senior care facilities, sadly people too often take their last breath far away from loved ones.[2] Or family is not able to be next to the dying until unconsciousness has set in. So there are no words from the dying person to be heard. Or remembered—which means that "last words" are often not recorded.

As I've mentioned, I was right there in our living room when my late wife, Bobbie, died. Our daughters, Missy and Julie, were close by. The night before, as I was resting from weeks of intense care for her—something I was honored to

---

2. This was especially tragic during the COVID-19 pandemic surges in 2020 and 2021.

do—Bobbie told my daughters, "I'm going to die tomorrow morning."

So early the next day, my late wife spoke her final words, and we were right there. She said to me, clearly and with a strong voice, "I love you so much." As you'd guess, this time, this place, these last words, are things we will never forget. Ever. But how deeply thankful we were—and are—that we had a chance to say goodbye and hear her words.

I've done a little research and have found some fascinating "last words" spoken by notorious or otherwise well-known people who were breathing their last within earshot of family and friends who recorded these words.[3]

Some even evoke a sardonic grin . . .

Convicted murderer Thomas J. Grasso used his last words to complain about his final meal. He said, "I did not get my Spaghetti-O's; I got spaghetti. I want the press to know this."

Marie Antoinette stepped on her executioner's foot on her way to the guillotine. Her last words: "Pardonnez-moi, monsieur."[4]

When Groucho Marx was dying, he let out one last quip: "This is no way to live!"

---

3. Chris Higgins, "64 People and Their Famous Last Words," Mental Floss, February 12, 2016, www.mentalfloss.com/article/58534/64-people-and-their-famous-last-words.
4. "Forgive me, sir."

As he was dying, Alfred Hitchcock said, "One never knows the ending. One has to die to know exactly what happens after death, although Catholics have their hopes."

Murderer James W. Rodgers was put in front of a firing squad in Utah and asked if he had a last request. He replied, "Bring me a bullet-proof vest."

Drummer Buddy Rich died after surgery in 1987. As he was being prepped for surgery, a nurse asked him, "Is there anything you can't take?" Rich replied, "Yeah, country music." [He died on the table.]

Richard B. Mellon, a multimillionaire, was the president of Alcoa. He and his brother Andrew had a little game of tag going for about seven decades. When Richard was on his deathbed, he called his brother over and whispered, "Last tag." Andrew remained "it" for four years, until he died.

Birth control advocate Margaret Sanger's last words were, "A party! Let's have a party!"

Or you and I may share feelings of sadness over the tragedy of lost people's final words . . .

Sir Winston Churchill's last words were, "I'm bored with it all."

Actress Joan Crawford yelled at her housekeeper, who was praying as she died. Crawford said, "Damn it! Don't you dare ask God to help me!"

As Benjamin Franklin lay dying at the age of 84, his daughter told him to change position in bed so he could breathe more easily. Franklin's last words were, "A dying man can do nothing easy."

Frank Sinatra died after saying, "I'm losing it."

Or like Bobbie, some die with tender words directed to those they love . . .

Actor Michael Landon, best known for *Little House on the Prairie* and *Highway to Heaven*, died of cancer in 1991. His family gathered around his bed, and his son said it was time to move on. Landon said, "You're right. It's time. I love you all."

Percy Grainger was an Australian composer who, with his dying words, told his wife Ella, "You're the only one I like."

Some who are dying are alert to the presence of God in the moment . . .

When Harriet Tubman was dying in 1913, she gathered her family around and they sang together. Her last words were "Swing low, sweet chariot."

William Henry Seward, U.S. secretary of state and architect of the Alaska Purchase, was asked if he had any final words. He replied, "Nothing, only 'love one another.'"

In chapter 8, you'll read about one of Nancy's dearest friends who died at the age of forty-two. Del Fehsenfeld, Jr. was a mentor to her and founded the ministry where she has been serving well over four decades. I mentioned Del in the last chapter—a first-person account of his seeing Heaven written from the vantage point of his daughter.

Nancy was also there, sitting close enough to him as he was dying. She heard Del's last, whispered words. Nancy leaned in, listened carefully, then quickly wrote down what he had said: "Lord, please bring back Your glory to Your church. Send the fire. Turn the hearts of Your people. May they know that You alone are God."

Can you imagine more powerful words?

If today you had a chance to formulate your final words, what would they be?[5]

TETELESTAI!

One dark afternoon on a rocky hill, suspended spread-eagle between earth and Heaven on a rough-hewn wooden cross, Jesus Christ offered the most remarkable final word anyone could ever speak.

The apostle John, who was right there and heard this word

---

5. This would be a cool discussion starter the next time your Bible study group meets.

with his own ears, recorded it in his gospel: "When he had received the drink, Jesus said, 'It is finished'" (John 19:30).

With that, Jesus said, "Father, into your hands I commit my spirit" (Luke 23:36). And then, as John tells us, Jesus "bowed his head and gave up his spirit" (John 19:30).[6]

Three words translated from a single Aramaic word (*tetelestai*) that stand in bold relief against all final words ever spoken.

"It is finished."

Beloved pastor and author Chuck Swindoll addressed the Savior's treasured, familiar last word like this:

It was a Greek expression most everyone present would have understood. It was an accounting term. Archeologists have found papyrus tax receipts with "Tetelestai" written across them, meaning "paid in full." With Jesus' last breath on the cross, He declared the debt of sin canceled, completely satisfied. Nothing else required. Not good deeds. Not generous donations. Not penance or confession or baptism or . . . or . . . or . . . nothing. The penalty for sin is death, and we were all born hopelessly in debt. He paid our debt in full by giving His life so that we might live forever.[7]

---

6. I have always imagined that Jesus was looking down at the people around the cross when He said, "It is finished." The work He had come to do on their behalf was completed. Then He looked up to His Father to whom He was commending His spirit. "I'm coming Home," Jesus was saying.

7. Charles R. Swindoll, *Jesus: The Greatest Life of All* (Nashville: Nelson, 2008), 224.

Every Jew hearing this word would have immediately recognized it as the Hebrew expression used in the sacrificial system of the old covenant.

Each year, on the Day of Atonement, the high priest would enter the temple and make a special sacrifice for the sins of the people of Israel. As soon as the priest had killed the animal, he would emerge from the place of sacrifice and declare to the waiting crowd, "It is finished," in Hebrew. In the ceremonial execution of this animal, all the sins of Israel were symbolically placed on the lamb that was killed, punished in their place.

Yet the Bible teaches that this sacrificial system was never really complete or finished because the ransom of that lamb was imperfect and temporary. But when Jesus died on the cross, He became the perfect and final sacrifice for all sin. The author of the book of Hebrews describes in chapters 9 and 10 how Jesus was the ultimate Lamb of God and how by His sacrifice, the work of forgiveness was finally complete.[8]

THE FINISHED LINE

The nineteenth-century British preacher Octavius Winslow summarized Jesus' moment of speaking His final word this way:

> The great truth, then, stands out like a constellation flaming in its own solitary orbit, that there never was but

---

8. Thanks to Doug Moen, PhD, for inspiring this powerful description.

one Man who could gaze with complacency upon His work, and, with His expiring breath, exclaim, "It is finished!" That man was the God-Man, Mediator, who, as the Son, and yet the Servant of the Father, relinquished his Throne for a Cross, that He might accomplish the Redemption, work out the salvation of His Church—the people given to Him of God—and who, on the eve of that Redemption, and with all the certainty of an actual Atonement, could thus breathe His intercessory petition to Heaven, "I have finished the work which You gave Me to do."[9]

◆ ◆ ◆

Several years ago, Nancy recorded a lengthy *Revive Our Hearts* podcast series on the last words of Christ. She called this collection of programs, "The Incomparable Christ."[10]

When she talked about "It is finished," she asked an important question about the antecedent to the word *it*. In other words, *what* exactly had been completed?

This is a remarkable list in case we're ever tempted to

9. Octavius Winslow, "Christ's Finished Work: A Sermon Delivered on Thursday Evening, April 4, 1861, at the Metropolitan Tabernacle, Newington," Christian Classics Ethereal Library, Spurgeon's Sermons, vol. 7, https://ccel.org/ccel/spurgeon/sermons07/sermons07.xxx.html. Because no one attending Spurgeon's Metropolitan Tabernacle in the mid-nineteenth century carried a smartphone that could capture their pastor's words, and because last week's sermons were not posted on the church's website to be replayed, I've often thought that if I had been there that morning when Winslow said this about the finished work of Christ, I would have wanted to raise my hand and ask him to repeat it. Slowly. I would have wanted to soak in the power and truth of what the pastor had just said one more time.

10. To be published in 2024 by Moody Publishers in book form by Nancy DeMoss Wolgemuth titled *Incomparable*.

think the crucifixion of Jesus was simply the story of a good man martyred because He was a good man and a posse of bad men wanted Him dead. It was more than that. A lot more.

Here's how Nancy explained what Jesus meant when He cried out, "It is finished."

The backstory is quite incredible:

- Every Old Testament prophecy throughout Jesus' earthly life and ministry was fulfilled/completed/accomplished . . . *Tetelestai!*—It is finished!
- Jesus had finished the work God sent Him to do on earth. He had succeeded in accomplishing the entire purpose for which He came to earth: *I have glorified You on the earth. I have finished the work which You have given Me to do* (John 17:4 NKJV). *Tetelestai!* It is finished!
- His suffering was ended. He had drained dry the cup of suffering—not a drop remained. He had finished it all. *Tetelestai!* It is finished!
- Sin's debt had been paid in full. The wages of sin is death . . . Jesus paid it all! *Tetelestai!* It is finished!
- The storm of God's wrath had been spent, had all been poured out on Christ as He became sin for us. *Tetelestai!* It is finished!
- God's eternal plan of redemption was now complete. It was perfect, complete, finished. *Tetelestai!* It is finished!
- The old covenant was finished. All kinds of sacrifices, shadows, symbols—in Christ, all had been fulfilled. *Tetelestai!* It is finished!

- The battle against Satan and sin had been won. Satan was defeated and stripped of his power. Next to every sin you and I have ever committed—"PAID IN FULL." At the cross, the battle against Satan/sin was won. *Tetelestai!* It is finished!

Nancy's overview of Jesus' final words is so helpful, isn't it?

Earlier I mentioned two meanings of the word *finish*. A homonym that could mean an exquisite sheen and the absolute conclusion of something.

When it comes to Jesus, I'd like to suggest that both definitions work.

THE OTHER "FINISH" . . . CELESTIAL GLORY

Back for a minute to the sparkling finish—the homonyms—of the eye-candied shine of my glistening car reminds me of the word *glory*. Like on that long-ago night when the shepherds looked and saw the angels and heard their pronouncement of the birth of Jesus, these ordinary men must have shielded their eyes from the incomprehensible glare. "Glory to God in the highest heaven" (Luke 2:14).

Jesus' use of the word *finished* draws a wonderful parallel to the radiant glory the sky must have featured on that holy night. And although the horrible scene at the cross surely looked to be anything but glorious, it was, in fact, exactly that.

The idea of the brilliantly displayed glory—the shiny finish—of Jesus also reminds me of the unsuspecting Paul of Tarsus, riding his horse to the city of Damascus for the purpose of persecuting Christians. The guy was literally knocked to the ground by a blinding light and a Voice from Heaven.[11]

The dazzling splendor of Jesus. A blinding sparkle. A brilliant finish, to be sure.

What an amazing goal for you and me. To *finish* well . . . with a beautiful, burnished, God-honoring *finish*.

I'm smiling at the thought of people squinting and shielding their eyes when they pass by our open caskets. The glory of the Lord is nothing to be hidden, even after we're gone. Can we envision a sign in front of our coffins that reads, "Let your light shine before others, that they may see your good deeds and glorify your Father in heaven" (Matthew 5:16)?

Nice finish.

---

11. The story is told in Acts 9.

FOUR

TWO FINISH LINE GUYS IN THE BIBLE

*And we know that in all things God works for the good
of those who love him, who have been called according
to his purpose.*

ROMANS 8:28

Twice in the Old Testament, we read of two men who had no personal finish lines. It's true. Enoch and Elijah went straight to Heaven without facing their own deaths: "Enoch walked faithfully with God 300 years and had other sons and daughters. Altogether, Enoch lived a total of 365 years. Enoch walked faithfully with God; then he was no more, because God took him away" (Genesis 5:22–24).

Why did this guy avoid the messiness of dying? Maybe the first phrase in two of these three verses give us a clue, right? It's repeated twice. *Enoch walked faithfully with God.* And the Lord gave him an end in a beautiful major key.

The second remarkable end belongs to the Old Testament prophet Elijah. In fact, this may be the coolest finish line in recorded history. Elijah and his protégé Elisha are literally on a stroll and chatting away. Listen to this: "As they were walking along and talking together, suddenly a chariot of fire and horses of fire appeared and separated the two of them, and Elijah went up to heaven in a whirlwind" (2 Kings 2:11).

Who wouldn't want one of those, right?

But there are many other ancient friends whose lives and eventual deaths are presented in the Bible. Here are a couple of my favorites, and even though these two lived a couple millennia apart from each other, there was something about them I want you to know, including their unique "calling" and their finish lines. And as unlikely as this may sound, maybe you and I can find ourselves tucked into their stories.

ABRAHAM

It was probably the fault of a thing they called flannelgraph when I was growing up. Images of Bible characters cut out of construction paper and soft cotton material glued to their backsides, and then slapped onto an easel-mounted board by Sunday school teachers who would explain the Bible stories by using these illustrations to visualize the point.

In this context as an eager little boy with a fuzzy buzz cut, I first heard the story of Abram as he was known before God changed his name to Abraham. I learned of the assignment God gave him to be the first of a lineage—the patriarch—of a people who would be known as the Israelites. Try as I might, identifying with this bathrobe-clad ancient people was a challenge. Was there anything about them that was worthy of my attention? For my young brain, there were more questions than answers.

Clearly the first conundrum was the news that God "called" Abram. What did a celestial assignment sound like? I knew what it meant when our mother called us in from the backyard for dinner. When I was a youngster, my thoughts may not have been able to comprehend the idea of the Creator of the universe calling a mortal—actually picking this man out from all others, communicating with him in a way he understood, and then orchestrating his life so specifically.

From the first time we see Abraham's name in Genesis 11 until his death recorded in Genesis 25, there's a lot we learn about him. Scripture tells us that Abraham was 175 years old when he died. Although it's tempting to chase the rabbit that scholars have pursued for a long time as to how and why Abraham and other Old Testament characters lived so long, I will not go there. For now, what's important is that Abraham was born, was given an assignment—a call—from God, married Sarai (later Sarah), fathered Isaac, moved a bunch of times, and then crossed his finish line.

If I may, let me return to the idea of calling . . .

What does this mean? You and I read that Abraham was called. Okay, fair enough. But is this a thing reserved for Bedouin wanderers who shuffle around the desert in sandals, carrying crooked sticks and leading sheep or punishing predatory animals who threaten their flocks. Or does "calling" still mean something now? And what does this have to do with preparing to cross our finish lines?

Well, since I've raised the issue, let me land the plane right here. Scripture tells us Abram was called. As were David, Esther, and Jesus. Actually, and here's big news—like them, you and I are also called. Yes, us. And this calling lasts from now until the end of our final straightaway.

Listen to this from the apostle Paul to his friend and protégé Timothy: "[God] has saved us and called us with a holy calling, not according to our works, but according to his own purpose and grace, which was given to us in Christ Jesus before time began" (2 Timothy 1:9 CSB).

ABRAHAM WAS CALLED. YOU AND I ARE CALLED. ALL THE WAY TO OUR FINISH LINE.

There you have it. Even if you and I aren't Israelites (the original called ones), God is still in the "calling business."

And how does "calling" work? And who, really, does the calling?

My friend Os Guinness has written about this. And here's what he said: "We cannot find God without God. We cannot reach God without God. We cannot satisfy God without God—which is another way of saying that our seeking will always fall short unless God's grace initiates the search and unless God's call draws us to him and completes the search."[1]

Don't you just love this? God is sovereign over all.

Abraham was called. You and I are called. Again, all the way to our finish line.

Calling is something God is capable of doing even before

---

1. Os Guinness, *The Call: Finding and Fulfilling the Central Purpose of Your Life* (1998; repr., Nashville: W Publishing, 2018), 15.

we're born. Listen to this from the prophet Jeremiah: "The word of the LORD came to me: I chose you before I formed you in the womb; I set you apart before you were born. I appointed you a prophet to the nations" (Jeremiah 1:4–5 CSB). Isn't this wonderful? Jeremiah's father's eye twinkled, his mother conceived, and a sovereign, loving God noticed. "I think I'll call that zygote a minister in My name," He must have said.

Incredible, right?

> MY FALLING HEAD OVER HEELS FOR THIS LOVELY LADY MAY NOT HAVE LOOKED LIKE A DIVINE APPOINTMENT TO THE CASUAL ONLOOKER. BUT IT WAS.

So, what does "calling" feel like? What if I never hear an audible voice or receive a message from a card-carrying prophet or a written note inside a floating bottle? How will I know?

Come with me to a go-to passage on this subject. One I have embraced for many years. It's from Paul to the first-century believers living in Philippi: "For God is at work within you, helping you want to obey him, and then helping you do what he wants" (Philippians 2:13 TLB).

Here's how this calling thing works. I pray and ask God to lead me when I'm facing a decision or a challenge. His Spirit is living inside me, and His ears are highly tuned. His first work is on my desires. I ask for His leading. His will. And He adjusts my "want to," matching His plan—His intentions—for me. Then He comes alongside and helps me execute His plan.

Game. Set. Match.

When I fell in love with Nancy in 2015, I was drawn to her. Even just a few weeks after our first date, my heart fluttered at the thought of her and when I was actually with her. I believe that being drawn to this woman and marrying her was a call. But I didn't embrace this only because I thought it was something that would please God. Surely that was the outcome, but He directed me to this plan by matching my heart with His will, by adjusting my affections to match His plan. My falling head over heels for this lovely lady may not have looked like a divine appointment to the casual onlooker. But it was.

When God called Abraham, I believe his heart was in a place where he wanted to gather his family and head to the Promised Land more than anything he could think of doing. Then as Abraham followed his own affections, God gave him the power to pull it off.

Back to the Genesis verse: "This is the length of Abraham's life: 175 years. He took his last breath and died at a *good old age, old and contented*, and he was *gathered to his people*" (Genesis 25:7–8 CSB, italics added).

What's interesting in following Abraham's consequential life is that in recording the moment of his death, Genesis 25 says only three things about this man: he died at a good old age, he was old and contented, and he was gathered to his people.

We're not told what Abraham died from, but I guess that living 175 years needs no further explanation. Right?

Isn't it interesting that Scripture says that Abraham's old age can be characterized by three things: good, contented, and communal? Neither you nor I will live to be 175 years old,[2] but this summary of the patriarch's death itemizes three characteristics we can embrace as we, like him, race toward our finish line.

A GOOD AGE

How many times a day do you use this word? *Good* usually proceeds the words *morning*, *afternoon*, *evening*, and *night*. We often use it to describe a boy, a meal, or a business plan. The word can even feel overused and benign. However, you may remember that during the week of creation, recorded in Genesis 1, the Lord God spoke this word to describe light, water, land, vegetation, the sun and the moon, fish, birds, and all living animals—including you and me. Good. Good. Good. Good. Good. And very good. Think of the enormity of all these things made from the voice of the Creator, and the highest form of praise was that they were good. Just simply good.

Does the creation narrative take the word *good* to the next level, giving it even more meaning when applied to the man Abraham? It does for me. Abraham lived to a *good* old age. Then he died. Finish line.

When Abraham died, the record shows that his old age was acceptable. It was good.

Isn't it interesting that the pinnacle of success is often referred to as "the good life"? We might imagine someone sitting in a hot tub, lifting something bubbly toward the sky and boasting to their friends, also right there soaking in the frothy water, "Ah, now *this* is the good life."

---

2. That's exactly a century older than me.

Good needs to mean a lot more than only good. When folks deliver spoken eulogies at our funerals, how satisfied will we be—although we won't hear any of it—if we're referred to as a good person? "Robert loved Jesus and the Bible. Robert did this. Robert did that. Robert married twice, fathered two daughters, started a business, wrote a few books, helped some people along the way . . . and Robert was a *good* man." How could I want anything more than this?

Suddenly this word used to describe Abraham at the close of his life sounds like a big deal. Because it is.

HE WAS OLD

It's interesting that Genesis 25:8 uses the word *old* twice with reference to Abraham.

When this book is published, I'll have been drawing air for seventy-five years. Because I have so many friends who are older than me, this doesn't sound ancient at all. But if I could sit down with eighteen-year-old Robert and forecast myself at that age, I'm sure I'd smile. *Man, that's old.*

Ever since Nancy was a little girl, she has aspired to one day be "a godly *old* lady." I've heard her say this many times. When asked what age she envisions, she'll say, "Oh, maybe eighty-five."[3]

So if I go with the numbers from the charts (see footnote),

---

3. The actuarial tables for women living in the United States say women die at eighty-one years old (CIA World Factbook 2022). Nancy would be beating the average by a few years. For men, the life expectancy is seventy-six years and eight months. In the "All" category, the average life expectancy in the U.S. is seventy-eight years and six months. See "List of Countries by Life Expectancy," *Wikipedia*, last modified May 27, 2022, https://en.wikipedia.org/wiki/List_of _countries_by_life_expectancy.

that means I have less than two years of life left. Actually—
and assuming I don't take up skydiving or eat fried pork
rinds every day for breakfast—I could dip into my family's
actuarial table based on my family history and also get an
idea of what my numeric end may be. When I bought life
insurance, the agent smiled at this information because in
buying this policy, I'm betting I'm going to die and the agent
is betting I'm going to live.

My dad died in 2002 at age eighty-seven. His dad was
ninety-two. My dad's mother was 105.[4] My mother died in
2010. She was ninety-four. My mother's mother passed away
when she was eighty-six. My mother's dad was just short of
his hundredth birthday.[5]

So even though Abraham's 175 years sounds crazy, I'm
sort of expecting to get old by today's standards—the average of the above legacy ages is ninety-four, eighteen years
more than the average. Of course, that's fine by me. I'm hoping the same for you.

For Abraham, "old" included a lot more than a sequence
of birthdays. Thinking through his life and experiences,
I'm amazed at how God used him in extraordinary ways to
accomplish this "call" on his life . . . for God's glory. I'm
guessing that Abraham was equally amazed.

When I die and the words "good old age" are used in my
eulogy, I'm trusting the same will be said of my years, however many there will be. Nancy's dad, Arthur DeMoss, only
lived to his fifty-third birthday, but God gave him a life just

---

4. I try to avoid exclamation marks when I write. But I came very close to
putting one here.

5. Ditto on wanting to use an exclamation point here.

long enough to leave an incredible legacy. A "long life" has more to do with what you and I do for Him, packing everything we can into the years we have, than the actual number of those years.

HE WAS CONTENTED

In 1907, the Carnation Company began using the slogan "Carnation Condensed Milk, the milk from contented cows." This slogan referred to the high-quality milk from happy cows grazing in the lush Pacific Northwest. Carnation used this trademark for decades, and it spawned a radio variety program titled "The Contented Hour," which featured entertainers such as Dinah Shore, Jane Powell, and Burns and Allen. *The George Burns and Gracie Allen Show*, which premiered on CBS television in 1950, was sponsored by Carnation.

Not only are Carnation's cows in a good place, Genesis 25 tells us that Abraham died "old and contented." In other words, when the patriarch died, he was very *old*—we've already covered this repeated word—and *contented*. Looking up in the Hebrew the word translated "contented," we find that it means "satisfied; completely and thoroughly gratified." I think of cuddling with my wife just before falling asleep at night. Peaceful. Lacking nothing in that moment. Contented.

Apparently, that was Abraham when he died. In fact, it wasn't just a word chiseled on his tombstone; it was part of the man's epilogue. Here are some "contented" moments in his life. In reviewing these, I'm reminded of similar markers in my own life. As you review Abraham's life, maybe you can identify a few "contented" moments in yours too. How many can you recall?

- **HOME SWEET HOME IN CANAAN** (Genesis 12): After traveling for more than three thousand miles, Abraham arrived in Canaan. Can you imagine the satisfaction (there's that word again) of answering God's call with a physical arrival in what would become the Promised Land? And let the idea of three thousand miles sink in. This is no set-the-cruise control trip on an interstate. It's walking. If you or I, as healthy and strong as we might be, would try this with only a bottle of water to carry, it would take seventy-two days, walking 24/7. I only mention this, envisioning the incredible joy—contentment on steroids—Abraham and his wife, Sarah, must have experienced when they arrived. Abraham . . . contented traveler.

- **IT'S A BOY** (Genesis 21): Abraham made love at age one hundred with his wife, age ninety. This wouldn't even be worth repeating for fear that it would be consigned to fable. Pure fiction. Except that the Bible records it as true. I'm picturing the centenarian holding his newborn son, Isaac, aloft, praising God for the miracle. Abraham . . . contented father.

- **A RAM IN THE BUSHES** (Genesis 22): It's like a prequel. A story before a story. A hint of incredible things to come. God speaks to Abraham and tells him to take his boy, his only son, Isaac, and sacrifice him. And just as Abraham is about to plunge a knife into his precious lad's body, an animal—the Bible calls it a ram—is sighted. Actually, the LORD speaks to Abraham to tell him of the male sheep, tangled in a bramble, that can take the place of his son as an atonement. This gripping account inspired many of my lessons in my years as a Sunday school teacher. The parallels with Jesus are manifold. Imagine the level of shock that must have enshrouded Abraham's mind. Shock, disbelief, submission, resignation, obedience, and then dazzling celebration. Abraham . . . contented believer.

♦ **FATHER OF THE GROOM** (Genesis 24): If Abraham is going to be the father of a nation, he'll need progeny beyond one son. Grandfathering would be essential. One of the Bible's most detailed accounts of a God-ordained, arranged marriage is the story—an abbreviated courtship, notwithstanding—of Isaac and Rebecca. Even though no detailed account of the wedding of these two can be found in Scripture, a traditional ceremony would have been inescapable. Since I have been one of the fathers at two weddings, deeply grateful for the choices my daughters made in mates, I can enthusiastically vouch for the joy. Abraham . . . contented father-in-law.

GATHERED TO HIS PEOPLE

One of the facts of life is that when you're our age, you attend a lot more funerals than weddings. In fact, I believe one of the most tragic results from the worldwide pandemic dubbed COVID-19 was that tens of thousands of people breathed their last in germ-free hospital rooms, surrounded by . . . masked-up hospital staff and not one person they knew. And the families and close friends of the deceased were unable to gather together to remember and grieve.

God willing, by the time you're reading this book, the word *pandemic* will have been consigned to the grim archives of world history.

Thankfully, by the sound of it, Abraham did not face this kind of isolation in his own death, or in the traditional service that followed. Once he was dead, he was gathered to his people.

The text could be referring to what the writer of the book of Hebrews calls "a great cloud of witnesses" surrounding us (Hebrews 12:1). Many scholars believe that this gathering—cloud—is made up of folks ahead of us in Heaven. The writer seems to be saying that those "saints" have an ability to celebrate us in our lives and deaths. So, Abraham's "gathering" is virtual. Almost like Zooming in on the moment, not able to be there in person at his memorial service but attending via broadband. Abraham's body was lovingly surrounded by "his people."

Forgive me if this sounds obvious, but you do know that once Abraham was dead, it was too late for him to love his gathered people. What he had done, the friendships he had established, during his lifetime was all there was going to be.

My late wife Bobbie's funeral was in November 2014. The First Presbyterian Church of Orlando, Florida, was brimming with a thousand friends. My immediate family alone numbered almost a hundred of them. These guests included members of our home church, couples who had been in our Sunday morning class, and women who were part of Bobbie's weekly Bible study. When I read that Abraham was "gathered to his people," I'm picturing this crowd, including thousands livestreaming,[6] as the gathered throng celebrating Bobbie's life.

Of course, my own Missy and Julie; their husbands, Jon and Christopher; and their five children—Abby,[7] Luke, Isaac, Harper, Ella—were there.

So there you have it, a summary of the Patriarch's life at the time of his death: old, contented, and surrounded by his people. What a textbook way to cross the finish line.

SIMON PETER

Like almost all Jesus' inner circle, Simon Peter was executed for what he believed. About Jesus.

Of all the disciples, I guess I identify most with Peter. Maybe not as outwardly brash as this guy, but I'm every bit as impetuous. Sometimes leading with my mouth rather than my thoughtfulness. Thankfully, the older I've grown, the more successful I've become at controlling myself.

So walk with me to one of the most important conversations Jesus had with this disciple. It took place on the shore of the Sea of Galilee, home base for many of the disciples.

Except for Judas, we don't know why the remaining disciples were not in this narrative, but we do know that seven of them were there: Simon Peter, Thomas, Nathanael, James, John, and two unnamed guys (John 21:2).

---

6. Just like the "cloud of witnesses" mentioned above. This cloud included a woman in Michigan, one of Bobbie's friends, named Nancy Leigh DeMoss. She was among them. How truly amazing this is for me to consider.

7. Abby's boyfriend, Benjamin Quirin, was also there. Ben and Abby married a year and a half later.

As the story unfolds in John 21, the writer cuts to the chase. The result of these fishermen's all-night net casting: "They went out and got into the boat, but that night they caught nothing" (verse 3).

Someone might quip that this is the very reason it's called "fishing" and not "catching." But these guys would not have been in the mood for levity. I'm sure of it.

As the morning sun was peeking over the horizon, Jesus shouted from the shoreline something you and I have said to discouraged—and likely angry—fishermen every time they come back from an excursion: "Friends," Jesus hollered out to them, "haven't you any fish?" (John 21:5).

If this doesn't conjure up at least a smile from you and me, we're not paying attention. Here's Jesus Christ. The Creator of Heaven and earth. The One who spoke these men into existence. The One who made the dry land and the sea. The One who made the fish and the water on which the disciples sailed and in which the fish swam. The One who, at that moment, ordered the earth to rotate ever so slightly, exposing the daybreaking sun so the men in the boat could see the form of a Man standing on the shore. This Man who did all these things, asking a question about their success on the lake. As though He didn't know full well how unsuccessful their trip had been.

Seriously?

But when they heard His naive-sounding query, they called back. "No."

Then Jesus threw out an idea that surely was received as pure contempt. The men obeyed anyway. Read it for yourself: "Throw your net on the right side of the boat and you will find some" (John 21:6).

Here is a sweet lesson in faith and trust, right in the middle of this story. These seasoned fishermen could have dissed the Rabbi. "What on earth does a holy man know about our trade?" What does the Man who claimed to be the Son of God, Creator of everything that lives and moves and has their being, know about it? Exactly.

Jesus told them to try something other than what they had been doing all night. So they did, and they were unable to haul it in because of the large number of fish. John breathlessly exclaimed to Peter, "It is the Lord!" (John 21:7).

Again, let these words sink in. Fishing all night. Nothing to show for it. Throw the nets on the other side? A crazy idea. Then—more fish than they can haul in. Let's call this a miracle. A clear realization that snagging all these fish was anything but ordinary.

After shouting the words, Peter, knowing that only Jesus could have done such a thing, did what we'd expect him to do. He stripped and jumped into the water, swimming like a bandit to see his friend, Jesus, the Miracle Worker, face-to-face.

By the time Peter arrived on the shore, there was a charcoal fire going with a fish already grilling.[8] Don't you just love this part?

Eventually the disciples joined Peter, dragging and heaving their catch—153 fish . . . "large" ones—onto the shore. These were likely tilapia, and their average weight would have been two pounds each. That's a lot. You do the math.

"Come and have breakfast," Jesus invited. And not only

---

8. Don't forget who we're talking about here. There may have even been a parsley garnish.

did He have fish they didn't catch, but He also had bread that He tore apart and gave to them. Sounds familiar, doesn't it?

What did the disciples say in the face of this incredible moment? They said nothing. Why? The text tells us: "None of the disciples dared ask him, 'Who are you?' They knew it was the Lord" (John 21:12).

In that moment, the sand on the Galilean beach became holy ground. The grains, like precious stones.

Jesus broke the silence and spoke. To Peter. His words must have cut deeply to the heart of this tough man. And as you and I read these words, they may sound like a change of subject. They're not. Listen carefully.[9]

"Simon . . . do you love me more than these?" Jesus asked.

"Yes, Lord. You know that I love you."

"Feed my lambs," Jesus responded.

Then He asked again, "Simon . . . do you love me?"

"Yes, Lord. You know that I love you," Peter said again.

"Take care of my sheep," Jesus said.

Then Jesus went for the trifecta. "Simon . . . do you love me?"

Because of the limitations of the English language, this sounds completely repetitive. But it's not. The first two times, Jesus uses the word *agape* for "love" in asking Peter. This is best defined as perfect, flawless, unfailing love. Even though Peter responds in the affirmative, he knows better. And he knows that Jesus knows better. Peter's denial on the night Jesus was convicted of something He had not done exposes Peter's flawed love for his Friend.

---

9. This whole conversation between Jesus and Peter is in John 21:15–17.

The third time, Jesus uses a different word for love. He returns to the word Peter uses. Jesus could have said, "I know you can't love Me with a perfect love. But are you My friend?"

Here's another way of looking at this powerful exchange: "Even the best efforts of our human love are but a shadow to the love of God. But holiness is not achieved by our own efforts to love—and thank God! True holiness derives from the love of Christ working within us. We can only love at all, because he first loved us (1 John 4:19)."[10]

Back on the shore, hunched over the fire, Jesus spoke to Peter. It was just the two of them. We don't know exactly how long it had been since Peter had lied about his relationship with Jesus, standing with strangers in a courtyard outside the place where Jesus was being cross-examined by Caiaphas the high priest (Luke 22:54–62). But it's certain that his lies were front and center in his mind as he and his Friend spoke.

Can you imagine the relief coming from Peter's heart? Finally, he had a chance to speak to the Someone he had so desperately wronged. You and I know this feeling, don't we?

And from Peter's point of view, this would have been a powerful, life-transforming exchange if it had stopped there. But it didn't. Listen carefully.

Having Peter's undivided attention, Jesus spoke of the eventual crossing of Peter's own finish line. To be candid, it does feel like a complete change of the subject.

Jesus continued: "Truly I tell you, when you were

10. Matthew Newsome, "Do You Love Me More Than These?" *Test Everything*, June 7, 2019, https://testeverythingblog.com/do-you-love-me-more-than-these-37735ffd7201.

younger, you would tie your belt and walk wherever you wanted. But when you grow old, you will stretch out your hands and someone else will tie you and carry you where you don't want to go. He said this to indicate by what kind of death Peter would glorify God" (John 21:18–19 CSB).

Suddenly you and I realize the importance of this seaside conversation. It's a setup. The miracle of the experiences Peter had just witnessed—his denial, the crucifixion, the empty tomb, the visitation of Jesus in a locked room, the invoking of the power of the Holy Spirit, the failed fishing trip, breakfast on the beach, and the bold challenge of Peter's love and certain death—was all a precursor to Jesus' loving, final prediction. And admonition about Peter's finish line.

Are you ready for it? Am I ready for it? We find Jesus' words to this bold disciple in the nineteenth verse of the narrative. It's all that you and I need to know about the time between now and our predicable and inescapable death. A death that we truly hope, as Jesus promised Peter, would literally glorify Him: "Jesus said this to indicate the kind of death by which Peter would glorify God. Then he said to him, 'Follow me!'" (21:19).

Here's your assignment, my reader friend. And it's a clear message from Jesus in the years leading up to our deaths. It's for you and me too. For us. Two simple words. Words for this life. And the next.

Follow me.

So how did Peter follow Jesus to his finish line?
One of the nifty features of looking into the life of

Simon Peter is that he recorded two letters of his own that appear toward the end of your New Testament. Here you and I get a chance to see the impact of his interaction with Jesus. Here's an example of what I mean: "Finally, all of you, be like-minded, be sympathetic, love one another, be compassionate and humble" (1 Peter 3:8).

This sounds a lot like the Savior's summation of the most important feature of His mission, delivered to His disciples but spoken in that sweet one-on-one with Peter: "A new command I give you: Love one another. As I have loved you, so you must love one another" (John 13:34).

HERE'S YOUR ASSIGNMENT. IT'S A CLEAR MESSAGE FROM JESUS IN THE YEARS LEADING UP TO OUR DEATHS. TWO SIMPLE WORDS. *FOLLOW ME.*

What did Peter's finish line look like? Actually, there's no biblical record of his death. There is, however, a lot of ink about what "church tradition" has to say about it. Got Questions Ministries, which comes alongside the church to help people find answers to their spiritually related questions, gives this answer to the question, "How did the apostle Peter die?"

The most commonly accepted church tradition is that Peter was crucified upside-down in Rome. Tradition says that, when Peter was put to death, he requested to be crucified on an inverted cross. [This would have been torture on top of torture.] The reason for his request was that, because he had denied his Lord, he did not consider himself worthy to die as Jesus had. Again, this is only a tradition, and the Bible doesn't confirm or deny the story. [From what we know, this sounds plausible.] . . .

Peter's love for Jesus and his desire to obey and glorify Him were evident throughout the rest of his life and ministry. For Peter to die a martyr's death clinging to the hope of heaven testifies to the courage, faith, patience, and perseverance of this great man of God who rejoiced to be counted worthy to die for the name of Jesus.[11]

Abraham's finish line. Simon Peter's finish line. Aren't you grateful for the example of these two men?

Me too.

---

11. "How Did the Apostle Peter Die?" Got Questions, accessed June 2, 2022, www.gotquestions.org/apostle-Peter-die.html.

FIVE

TEMPLE CARE

*Have you considered that your greatest ministry may
be at the end of your life? The greatest fruitfulness
may be in how you and I die.*

Kevin DeYoung, "Heaven Is Gain"[1]

You're likely familiar with the concept of our bodies being compared to physical structures. Buildings. In fact, the Bible calls these houses you and I live in "temples."

Of course, there are serious reasons why these physical frames we are in right now are compared to religious structures. Like churches or synagogues. Two come to mind at the moment.

---

1. In November 2008, then the pastor of the University Reformed Church in East Lansing, Michigan, Dr. Kevin DeYoung preached a sermon called "Heaven Is Gain." His crisp wisdom and clear insights about death and Heaven are so helpful. I commend this entire talk to you: https://christcovenant.org/sermons/heaven-is-gain.

WORSHIP

Often when churches or synagogues or mosques or temples are referenced on newsfeeds, they're called "Houses of Worship."

The apostle Paul approached the idea of comparing our flesh and blood to brick and mortar like this:

> Do you not know that your bodies are temples of the Holy Spirit, who is in you, whom you have received from God? You are not your own; you were bought at a price. Therefore honor God with your bodies. (1 Corinthians 6:19–20)

For the sake of our conversation in the first part this chapter, I'm going to focus on the physical rather than the spiritual implications of the metaphor.

Think of the structure you now find yourself sitting inside. It may be your home, an airport, or a coffee shop. Or you may be reading this under one of those beach cabanas you can rent overlooking the ocean. If so, color me a little jealous. Regardless of when it was built or the purpose of the building, the absolute truth is that it's deteriorating. As we speak. The paint is fading. The wood is rotting. Or insects of every stripe are bowing their tiny heads and saying grace.

This is also true of my physical body as I run/jog/crawl to my finish line. And as you run toward yours. Early in our lives, this fact was not front and center. Now it is.

And what does this physical deterioration look like?

There are a lot of finish line issues that remind us of our slowly deteriorating structures, like sitting on the edge of our bed when we awaken early in the morning, before we take our first steps. Because I have a tendency toward chronic anemia, my doctor encouraged me to do this. "I don't want to read in the papers that you killed yourself doing a face-plant," he said with a serious grin.

The past several years for me have been nothing if not an absolute reminder of the fragility of my physical house. This is first revealed when the kind nurse asks me to take my clothes off in the pre-op room. Like you, I have a closet full of clothing. Everything from a college sweatshirt to a tuxedo provides a fashion coating for my body. I'm fond of using "soft clothes" so I can leisurely curl up on the couch to watch a movie with my wife. I also have appropriate clothing if I'm headed to a formal engagement. But standing in my bare feet on the cool floor of a doctor's office, with nothing on but a cotton gown that actually covers very little of my sagging frame, I am very aware of this deteriorating house.

AGING GRACEFULLY

I suppose there are not two women I've ever known who aged more gracefully than my mother, Grace, and her sister-in-law, Lois Dourte. Grace stepped into Heaven in 2010 at the age of ninety-four. As of this writing, Lois is ninety-one. And vibrant.

As I think about my own aging house and the deterioration that comes with it, I'm heartened by the way these women didn't seem to succumb to the temptation to let their houses collapse, in spite of the advancing years.

Notice, I'm making a distinction between the house and the temple. This is not a difference without a distinction. These are not the same. Our "house" is the physical structure. As you sit there reading this, you have 206 bones,[2] 360 joints, and 640 muscles in your house. You have 15 feet of intestines, 60 thousand miles of blood vessels, and 90 thousand miles of nerves.[3] All of this begins to form in our bodies at the moment of our conception. This is too amazing to even comprehend.

King David certainly got it right when he announced that you and I are "fearfully and wonderfully made." And then he added, "Your works are wonderful, I know that full well" (Psalm 139:14).

As we age our bones get porous and break. Our joints weaken. Our intestines get twisted and blocked. That's our house.

But what about our temple? Our very own house of worship?

The houses belonging to Grace and Lois weakened with age. Happily their temples—their houses of worship—did not fade. These were women of the Word. Time in their Bibles was a fixture in their schedules, and they loved God and embraced the salvation that only Jesus provides. When alone, they could be overheard humming or singing a favorite hymn. When they spoke to family and friends, their spirits and words were predictably kind, encouraging, and upbeat.

---

2. Some say 213, depending on how our vertebrae are counted.
3. "The Nervous System: More Than 90,000 Miles of Sensations," Visual Dictionary, accessed June 2, 2022, www.ikonet.com/en/visualdictionary/static/us/the_nervous_system.

They smiled a lot. These temples, by God's grace, remained strong. And beautiful.

Okay, how's my house?

Well, it's like yours. Wrinkles and aches are plentiful.

And how are our temples? Our very own places of worship? And do we have someone at the top of our contacts who can help? Thankfully, I do. For both.

DR. LOWELL HAMEL

When I moved to Michigan in 2015, I began to look for a doctor. A general practitioner (GP) who would be the guy I'd go to for standard-issue annual physicals, someone who could quarterback anything that might pop up beyond normal stuff.

I asked Nancy if she thought her GP might be able to make room for another patient. She told me she thought he had a full load, but she promised to ask. She did, and Dr. Lowell Hamel agreed to one meeting with me to talk.

If the goal was to find a professional to help me manage the care of my physical "house," I could not have wished for anyone better than Dr. Hamel. This professional was not only fully available, but he and I shared congruent experiences with non-Hodgkin lymphoma cancer and COVID-19. Both of these Lowell contracted before I did. And he showed me how to courageously deal with them.

In fact, I had the honor of being his first patient for my annual physical after we both had finished our final chemo treatments and were waiting to see if our hair would ever return. It did.

Although I'm confident that no professional distance has been breached, I can say that having this man beside me has been one of the greatest blessings of this season. His friendship and generosity have been pure joy.

This is the "handyman" the Lord has blessed me with as I manage the care of my "house." And I could not be more grateful for his faithful care.

DR. DAVID SWANSON

Another doctor in my life has his graduate degree in theology, not medicine. David Swanson has also appeared on the first page of my contacts since 2003, and he has helped me take care of the temple. Over the years, I have had the joy of being "shepherded" by these skilled and gracious men.

In 2012, when Bobbie was diagnosed with Stage IV ovarian cancer, David offered—promised—to be my "wingman." In fact, before Bobbie's surgery on February 14, David came to the hospital in Orlando. He, Bobbie, my daughter Missy, and I gathered in a tight circle in the main lobby. There David earnestly prayed. He invoked the presence of the Great Physician to give the surgeon wisdom and skill and to help my wife make it through with "little or no pain."

Bobbie later confessed to me that although she sincerely appreciated David's request regarding the pain, she was a little dubious about the "little or no pain" part. Six and a half hours later, Bobbie's oncologist gave Missy and me the diagnosis. And the prognosis.

Bobbie, Missy, and I spent the next three days at the

MD Anderson Cancer Center. As Bobbie began the healing process from a radical procedure that included the longest incision I'd ever seen on a person's tummy, multiple doctors and nurses visited. Every time they came to her room, they'd ask her, "On a scale of zero to ten, what would you say your pain level is?"

> MY SINCERE SUGGESTION IS THAT YOU FIND YOUR OWN HANDYMAN AND CARETAKER. AS SOON AS YOU CAN.

The first time they asked, I remember Bobbie wondering if she had to answer the question because she had no pain. They said yes. So from then on, she'd just smile. "Oh, I'd say zero." The Lord so kindly answered David's specific prayer.

From the summer of 2004 until I moved to Michigan in 2015, David Swanson was my pastor and dearest friend. There aren't enough superlatives I could write to amply describe how precious this man was to me.

In chapter 8, I talk about making plans for my funeral. It would probably not come as a surprise to you that David Swanson will be one of the pastors to speak.

If Lowell Hamel was the handyman for my "house," David Swanson was the sexton of my "temple."

Since you and I are friends, my sincere suggestion is that you find your own handyman and caretaker. As soon as you can.[4]

---

4. My editor asked me for some practical help in finding relationships like this. Church will always be the best place to find like-minded friends. Don't be in a hurry to leave when the services are finished. Hang out. Talk. Ask good questions. Also, I've discovered that texting can be a terrific way to troll for possible friendships. Send someone you know a Bible verse. See if they respond. If they

THE FRIENDLESS MALE

In my recent book *Gun Lap*,[5] I talk about the challenges of getting older both physically and relationally.

The book triggered many important conversations between me and other men my age. One of the common refrains was the challenge of developing and maintaining meaningful friendships during the season of getting older, heading toward our finish line. In fact, the account of older, lonely men taking their lives is a familiar, tragic refrain. Statistically, men my age lead the pack.[6]

Just a few months ago I had a prolonged conversation with an old friend. Even though some of our talk related to publishing things, a big chunk of it was good chatter among buddies. One of the remarkable things this guy recently did was move from a major metropolitan area to a relatively small town. The reason is that this community was home to his university alma mater. He and his fraternity brothers, who had, out of necessity after graduation, scattered around the county to seek their fortunes, were all retired now. And they got tired of trying to maintain their lifetime

---

do, a few days later send them another. And so forth. You'll be surprised how this can turn out to be a good way to find brothers and sisters who are looking for someone like you.

5. Robert Wolgemuth, *Gun Lap: Staying in the Race with Purpose* (Nashville: B&H, 2021).

6. According to the National Council on Aging, suicide is one of the leading causes of death in the United States, affecting men and women of all ages. Older adults are especially vulnerable to suicide for a number of reasons, ranging from grief over the passing of loved ones to chronic illness. The NCOA concludes that "men 65 and older face the highest overall rate of suicide" ("Suicide and Older Adults: What You Should Know," NCOA, September 7, 2021, https://ncoa.org /article/suicide-and-older-adults-what-you-should-know).

friendships virtually. So they all moved back to their college town.

As this friend was telling me about the pure joy of reconnecting with his college chums, I admit to feeling a wave of jealousy. I even said so. In fact, right now, except for Nancy, there isn't a single adult in my life living close by that I knew before 2015. All these people are new friends. And even though this has been sweet, I really miss men with whom I share history.

Even though it's not the same as getting together face-to-face, can I encourage you to create a "text thread" with a handful of old friends? At the recommendation of a relative, I did this. And almost every day there's some kind of communication with these college classmates. It may be sharing a funny thing about getting old—and there are plenty of these—or news about a child or grandchild or a health update or a prayer request.

Again, this is not the same as actually being together, but this text thread is precious. We even have occasional video calls that have been great fun.

Talking about Lowell Hamel and David Swanson and old college classmates reminded me of another close friend. Since we were both leaders in the Christian publishing world and because that world is quite small, this guy and I had many occasions to be together. Multiple meals and meetings put us in the same space often.

Brian was just a few years my junior and was one of my favorite friends in the business. His brilliance, his low-key manner, his thin but winsome smile, sparkling eyes, and his ability to confidently articulate complex things were among the things I loved about him. Mostly, I loved his dry sense of humor. Even looking back on a particularly prickly meeting we both participated in, this man had the skill of lifting both our spirits above the malaise and even chuckling about it. Later.

Because Brian played an important role in my writing, I mentioned him in the acknowledgments of one of my books, thanking him for his friendship, support, and professional contribution to the work. In late June 2019, I received a call from a man who was a mutual friend of this guy and me. His first words were, "Have you heard the terrible news?"[7]

Then he told me that this friend was dead. And he had likely taken his own life.

I could not believe it then. Frankly, I still cannot.

You may already know this, but the statistics of men in their sunset years who take their own lives are staggering. As an aging man, I find this troubling. Awful. Yet, strangely understandable.

It would come as no surprise to you that women are in a different canoe. If you're a woman, you know this to be true. Many women have many friends. Men, not so much.

Now your kids are grown, maybe married, likely no longer living in your home, and have plenty of adult friends of their own. But what about you? Where are the parents of your kids' friends? The ones you sat next to on the sidelines at soccer games on weekends?

It may feel more natural for you as a woman to reach out to other women than it is for a man to reach out to his

---

7. I'm not a big fan of conversations that start this way. You?

friends, and you need to do it. Again, church is ground zero for cultivating friendships with other women.

My wife Nancy's ministry produces some wonderful resources that women can use as a catalyst to gather with friends. We receive reports from around the world of how women are connecting with each other, of how especially older women—veterans in life's race—are finding ways to encourage younger women.[8]

So my point here is that in this season you ought to take another look at your friendships. As you scan the landscape of people you've worked with or known well, who among them stands tall?

> TO FINISH YOUR RACE ALONGSIDE AT LEAST ONE MAN, ONE SOUL BROTHER. ONE WOMAN, ONE SOUL SISTER. THAT'S THE PURPOSE.

And the purpose of this would be? you may wonder.

To finish your race alongside at least one man, one soul brother. One woman, one soul sister. That's the purpose.

WHAT'S THIS FOR?

Many years ago, when Bobbie and I had a small second home in Charlotte, North Carolina, just a few blocks from my daughters and their growing families, I scheduled a regular Friday lunchtime with my two grandsons. It was wonderful.

---

8. Nancy's landmark book and study guide *Adorned: Living Out the Beauty of the Gospel Together* have been a great encouragement to women, especially older women who are loving and mentoring younger women in a "Titus 2" kind of way. (Chicago: Moody, 2018).

For almost seven years, once a month, we had our Friday meeting with two goals for these times.

The first was to try not to go back to the same restaurant twice. The second goal was to visit the local hardware store—Renfrow's Hardware & General Merchandise. (You already love this place because of its name, don't you?) The operation was established before the turn of the century, 120-plus years ago. It was the kind of old hardware store that smelled exactly like . . . an old hardware store.

After Luke, Isaac, and I enjoyed our lunch, we'd walk the aisles of this classic treasure in downtown Matthews. You'd think that with the advent of massive, big-box stores, places like this wouldn't survive. But these guys have. The floors were wooden, and they creaked when we walked on them. A thin layer of dust rested on almost everything. But that was part of the charm. The strong smell of fertilizer met us just inside the front door. In the paint section, turpentine's unmistakable aroma bathed the air.

Luke, Isaac, and I played a game. As they walked up and down the aisles, scanning the stuff laid out on the shelves, they'd look for something they didn't recognize. A tool whose usefulness was completely unknown to these boys. They'd pick it up and ask me, "What's this, Grandaddy?" And I'd tell them.[9]

In this project of evaluating your closest allies to help you take care of your house and temple, ask yourself these questions: *What is this friend for? What do they give me? What do I offer to them?* Good questions with important answers.

---

9. I know this really sounds old school, but I believe that if a boy knows his way through a hardware store, he will be set for life.

WHERE TO FROM HERE?

In buttoning up this chapter, I'm aware that you and I have covered several potentially disparate things. I'd love for you to think of this chapter—and the whole book—as a visit to Luby's cafeteria.

You start your journey with your tray, sliding it down the clean chrome rails. As you move along, you see various selections. Some look good and tasty, others not so much. You set the appetizing things on your tray, the others you leave alone and scoot by them.

Here's a quick summary:

- You and I need a handyman and a sexton. Having someone on speed dial for your physical heath and a trusted person on speed dial for your spiritual well-being would be brilliant.
- Scan your friends as though they're standing in a lineup. Pick out one or two and begin to focus your attention on building a deep friendship. *What's the use for this?* you may wonder. *What's it for?* Pour yourself into one or two people and you'll find out.

Now, speaking of Renfrow's, let's talk some nuts and bolts. Essentials that must be in place before you're gone.

SIX

NUTS AND BOLTS

You may not be a do-it-yourself person. A screwdriver and a hammer may be the extent of the tools you own. That's just fine. Actually, Nancy has often reminded me that if there were any other tools at her home, her daddy would not have known where or what they were. Yet he was one of the most admired Christian leaders of his day.

The fact that over the years I've owned more than a screwdriver and a hammer is not a qualitative statement. It does not—by any stretch of your wildest imagination— make me a better man than Arthur DeMoss.

However, the truth is that I've owned a veritable truck-load of tools. Some that needed an electrical outlet, some that were gas-powered, and many that just needed my arms and hands to make them work.

The title of this chapter gives a clue as to where you and I are headed. We're going to talk about the blueprint of your death. By that I mean the design and the nitty-gritty of the tools that you're going to need to have in place to make sure your demise doesn't become a horrendous burden to your surviving loved ones.

Before going any further, I'm going to dare to insult you by starting with four must-haves. The potential insult may come when you read these next paragraphs. Like, you may say out loud, "Who on earth doesn't already know this, Robert?"

As I said, forgive me in advance, but I'm going to risk insulting your intelligence by forging ahead.

Here are the four essentials.

A PERSONAL PHYSICIAN

We talked about this in the last chapter, but it bears repeating here. You may refer to this person as your PCP (primary care physician) or GP (general practitioner) or family practice doctor, but this person is not optional equipment. Not at your age.

When Bobbie was diagnosed in February 2012 with stage IV ovarian cancer, my Missy and I sat with Bobbie's oncologist in a small conference room immediately following six and a half hours of surgery. She told us what she had found: "cancer throughout her midsection, spread out on her organs like peanut butter."

Missy and I were stunned. Speechless. Thankfully, the doctor kept talking. She told us that as soon as Bobbie healed from the dramatic violation of her body under the knife, six rounds of chemo should come next. Right away. We nodded, believing that her counsel was worth following. Then she added something. In fact, it was more of a gentle warning. "When this news gets out to your family, your friends, and acquaintances—even folks you don't know—you're going to get more advice than you can imagine. It'll be an avalanche."

Boy, was she ever right about that.

Our phones and email in-boxes quickly filled with advice. From homeopathic solutions to alternate medicines to massive overdoses of organic substances, well-meaning and kind people contacted us with information. And recommendations on websites we should check out. Again, please don't misunderstand, just in case you were one of them. I was then and continue to be deeply grateful for the love that was expressed by these "surefire solutions" to our situation.

But let me take you back to the conference room where Bobbie's doctor alerted Missy and me to what she found. The first thing that came to my mind was a sports analogy.

"Regardless of what we hear from anyone in any place," I said to her, "you will always be our quarterback."

She nodded and smiled. Even though this particular doctor was quite new to us, we had heard rave reviews about her track record with women's cancers. The trust in her that I expressed that day was not random. And over the next thirty months of seeing multiple other doctors and undergoing procedures, even a horrendous clinical trial, this doctor was the one under center. For every play. I never regretted hiking her the ball.

Having a primary doctor/quarterback in Orlando calling the plays, including audibles, was a good idea. So when I moved to Michigan at the age of sixty-seven, one of the first things I did—after I unscrewed the Florida license plate on my car and affixed a new Michigan one in its place in the bitter cold—was to find a PCP.

For me.

This was one of the smartest things I've ever done. In January 2016, I could have passed as a much younger man, almost completely free of any besetting diseases. Except for an appendix episode and a few knee surgeries, I was a healthy, regular-exercising guy. But the next few years became a carousel of sobering diagnoses. From kidney trouble to two unrelated cancers, multiple scans, biopsies, and appointments with literally a dozen different specialists meant the possibility of being medically overwhelmed. But I had the luxury of having a medical Tom Brady. A Peyton Manning.[1] A first-string quarterback.

On speed dial.

Today, even though I occasionally shoot my doctor an encouraging text or a Bible verse that will lift his spirits, I usually approach him with questions or to fill a prescription by way of a MyChart account that reaches him and his team without intrusion. And because he's my very own go-to guy and he knows me, he gets back to me. Usually within twenty-four hours. Sometimes faster.

Having this man as my doctor has been a massive blessing. He makes me feel safe. Like so many things I'll mention in this book, there's nothing more helpful in finding a perfect field commander than recommendations from others who have their own quality quarterback.

---

1. A Joe Burrow. A Patrick Mahomes. A Josh Allen. Etc.

A TRUSTWORTHY ATTORNEY

There are going to be times when a competent lawyer will be a great backstop. It may be that your need for such a professional will be infrequent. If you're leasing an apartment or buying a new house, it's good to have someone you can call for legal advice.

To locate the best attorney for our legal needs, Nancy and I informally agreed to the following checklist. See what you think.

* Someone who is a Christian. The Bible is clear about this thing called "stewardship." That means everything we "own" belongs to the Lord. The big decisions we make regarding the way we handle our lives and our stuff are a critical part of our faith. We believe our attorney needs not only to agree that this is essential but also to embrace the same for herself.

* A person who is younger than we are, enhancing the chances that our lawyer will outlive us. This is important in the time between now and our deaths because they can have the documents handy for additions we make now and for its official execution when we're dead.

* A person who comes highly recommended. It's the same as when you're looking for good employees for your business—or a mate, for that matter. Finding a highly qualified lawyer should include asking your trusted friends who they would recommend.

+ A no-obligation conversation with the prospective lawyer. Before moving ahead with our professional affiliation with her lawyer, Nancy and I engaged in an in-depth conversation. We interviewed her; she interviewed us. The attorney-client relationship is both legally and practically "a thing." We wanted to be sure.

Some of my best friends are lawyers. I'm not kidding. And speaking of kidding, I do have a substantial reservoir of jokes about these folks. I've told them some, and each time they laugh along with me.

But having a great lawyer is not a laughing matter. It's serious.

My personal lawyer story starts in Nashville, where we lived for seventeen years. I met this man when he visited my Sunday school class—which would have been around 1990. And because he told me how much my teaching—as a volunteer layperson—meant to him and how it had impacted his life, he promised to never send me an invoice for his professional help. For more than thirty years, and a lot of legal work on my behalf, I never paid him. Anything, because he never asked.

Now, to be clear, I told him that if I ever was able to help him professionally, I'd return the favor. And, as it turned out, he wrote a book in 2007 about the Duke lacrosse team fiasco.[2] I stepped in as his agent and found a publisher and did not bill

---

2. Nader Baydoun and R. Stephanie Good, *A Rush to Injustice: How Power, Prejudice, Racism, and Political Correctness Overshadowed Truth and Justice in the Duke Lacrosse Rape Case* (Nashville: Nelson, 2007).

him for my commission. We bartered. Sort of like the pilgrims swapping beaver pelts with Native Americans for maize.

Since then, on matters that didn't need a Michigan license to practice, this friend has been by my legal side. But since a lot of what Nancy and I have needed since November 2015 has required state certification, we did find another attorney. And she has been fantastic. Like my other attorney, she makes me feel safe.

Our lawyer has helped Nancy and me create an estate plan.

Just the mention of these two words—"estate plan"—may throw you off. You may remember the syndicated show that ran for eleven years from 1984 to 1995 called *Lifestyles of the Rich and Famous*. The host, Robin Leach, had one of those captivating British accents and ushered viewers into the homes, yachts, and private jets of billionaires around the world. When I just mentioned "estate plan," you may have smiled, thinking to yourself, *Oh, nice, Robert. Let me speak with my butler and see if he can help me locate a copy of my estate plan somewhere here in my two-story library.*

But that's not it at all. It's basic. And understandable. And important. In fact, to show you what I mean, I asked our friend and counsel Lisa Hagenauer-Ward to send me a summary of what an estate plan needs to include. Regardless of your financial situation, this portfolio of things will be a runway for you and your family, both now and when you're incapacitated or dead. Here it is—abridged and in plain language so your mind doesn't glaze over with these details.[3]

---

3. What I have written here is only meant to be a thin start. An overview. I highly recommend www.kingdomadvisors.com, where you can click on the

LAST WILL AND TESTAMENT AND/OR REVOCABLE LIVING TRUST

The first time I created a will was in 1972, soon after our first child was born. And over the years, as my life and obligations changed, this document was updated appropriately.

Going through old files, I discovered that my will needed some serious updating. As you may know, far too many people our age die without a will. According to some surveys, almost 70 percent of us don't have one.[4]

What this means is that, upon your death, if you don't have a will, the state will step in and make decisions about the disposal of your assets. Imagine someone you've never met—and, because you're dead, will never meet—calling these shots without your input. How much better to be able to determine the destination of your money and stuff and what happens with your heirs and the charities you loved and supported while you were alive![5]

- A will provides instructions for distributing your assets to your surviving mate, your children, and grandchildren at the time of your death. A will alone does not necessarily avoid probate court administration.
- A revocable living trust allows for management of financial matters during your lifetime and then at your

---

"Find an Advisor" tab. It will give you information on a qualified attorney, accountant, or financial planner in your area.

4. See Reid Kress Weisbord and David Horton, "Significant Figures: 68% of Americans Do Not Have a Will," The Conversation, May 19, 2020, https://the conversation.com/68-of-americans-do-not-have-a-will-137686.

5. I highly recommend Ron Blue's *Splitting Heirs: Giving Your Money and Things to Your Children without Ruining Their Lives* (Chicago: Northfield, 2004).

death. If assets properly flow through your trust, probate court administration is avoided and the privacy of your planning is protected.

♦ Whether you need trust planning or whether a will without trust planning will meet your needs may be less about how much you have and more about the types of assets you have and your need to have control or flexibility in your planning. A detailed discussion of your family, needs, and objectives with your attorney will help you determine which types of planning works best for you.

DURABLE POWER OF ATTORNEY FOR PROPERTY

This document designates another person you choose to act on your behalf during your lifetime regarding accounts and assets in your name if you are unable to do so. This allows the important details of your life to continue even if you are incapacitated.

HEALTH CARE POWER OF ATTORNEY

This document appoints someone to make health care decisions on your behalf in the event you are unable to do so. It helps avoid family conflicts and the need for court intervention while helping ensure that your wishes regarding your health care are honored. It's sometimes referred to as a health care proxy or a patient advocate designation. In addition to addressing medical care, this document may deal with matters such as organ donation, final disposition of your body, pain management, and end of life treatment.

LIVING WILL

This document expresses your wishes regarding life-sustaining treatment when death is imminent or you are suffering from a terminal illness. It's often called an "advanced directive."

The best part of the exercise for Nancy and me with Lisa was answering her questions regarding important tactical issues. Again, there's really nothing fun about it, but imagine what it accomplishes in answering questions your survivors will surely have after you're gone. It also can be a helpful— and sometimes challenging—exercise now for you and your mate, as well as your children and grandchildren who need to know what you have decided to do or the plans you have made. Things like:

◆ Who's who? In chapter 8, we're going to talk about planning for your funeral, including who you want to take part in the service. It's just as important to list in one easily accessible place the complete contact information for the members of your family, your pastor, your attorney, your accountant, your financial planner, and your insurance agent. You also will want to list your passwords so your loved ones will be able to access your electronic devices.[6] And now is a good time to decide who will help to manage the process. In the last chapter, we talked about having a quarterback for your medical needs. Here's a spot for another quarterback. Who is the person you trust to help oversee all

---

6. Nancy and I use a program called LastPass to manage all our passwords. It's terrific. She has access to all my passwords. Nancy reminded me of one yesterday when my computer was down.

these things? Is it someone your whole family trusts? This is so important.

• Because I have been involved in ministries in one way or another my whole life, I've seen these ministries be blessed by folks who include "the Lord's work" in their will. How good would it be for you to prepare investments in worthwhile efforts that will provide blessings after your death? Jesus told an unforgettable story about stewardship—what happens to what we leave behind when we're gone.[7]

• Who gets what? Technically called beneficiary designations, this document identifies things you own—from your house to your jewelry to your baseball card collection to your piano to your golf clubs—and specifies who will receive these when you're gone. It's important to discuss with your attorney the proper way to designate beneficiaries of your various assets so that your wishes are honored and your good intentions don't lead to bigger problems because your designations weren't done properly. There's nothing wrong with discussing this with them before you die. Your children may welcome having an extra car but may have little interest in your spoon collection or your duck-hunting paraphernalia. Why would you "bless" them with things they don't want? As Lisa told us, uncertainty leads to conflict. You and

---

7. Matthew 25:14–28 tells the story of a master who left different amounts of money to three servants before going on a long journey. The indelible point of the story is that those servants were charged with taking good care of what the master had given them. Two were worthy. One was not. Good stewardship.

I have seen how this has played out in other families, haven't we? It's not pretty.

A QUALIFIED ACCOUNTANT

When Nancy and I married in 2015, she was fifty-seven. I was sixty-seven.

As you'd guess, we had each used our own accountant leading up to our nuptials. Before our wedding we discussed our thoughts regarding this professional. As it turned out, because my personal accountant was also the CPA for my business and his fees were fair, it made sense to keep his services for both of us.

Even though I consider myself to have at least an average level of intelligence about financial things, keeping up with tax laws and doing annual filings on my own have never been a temptation. Years ago, I even agreed to a couple one-year terms of office as the treasurer of my homeowners association, and all went well. But that was essentially managing a checkbook. Beyond that I'm as lost as last year's Easter egg.

Having a true professional look over matters like annual IRS filings should not be negotiable. A qualified accountant and smart financial planner are essential.

A FINANCIAL PLANNER

Many years ago, by way of a mutual friend, I was introduced to a man named Ron Blue. Because of his stellar reputation in the financial services business and his strong testimony of love for Christ, and because I was a publisher and thought he might be interested in writing a book, we became friends.

The result was a book called *Master Your Money*, which to date has sold more than three quarters of a million copies, including a few revisions to keep up with the changing laws related to investments and taxes.[8] This book will continue to be a classic for many years to come.

My friendship with Ron has continued, including working with him on more books and enjoying a very special relationship with a group Ron helped to launch called Kingdom Advisors (KA). This is an association of thousands of Christian financial planners, attorneys, and CPAs. On KA's website you will find this statement: "A lot of Christian advisors don't actually have a process to deliver biblical advice to clients. We've helped thousands of financial professionals by offering a simple, step-by-step process to engage clients with biblical principles."[9]

Who wouldn't want to have allies like this?

When Nancy and I married, we sensed the need to find a new financial planner who could help us work through some of the challenges of blending our lives and finances together. As is true of the process of selecting all these professionals, first-person endorsements are the best way to sort through the choices and find the best planner. For you.

One of Nancy's good friends, also a Michigan resident,[10]

---

8. Ron Blue, *Master Your Money: A Step-by-Step Plan for Experiencing Financial Contentment* (Chicago: Moody, 1986, 1991, 1997, 2004, 2016).

9. Kingdom Advisors, https://kingdomadvisors.com.

10. It will save you some headaches if you find a CFP headquartered in the same state where you live.

suggested we contact a firm located only an hour and a half from us. We made a phone call and scheduled an appointment. Before the first consultation was finished, Nancy and I had a sense that these folks would be a good fit for us. On the drive home, we prayed. We asked the Lord for wisdom. We soon made the decision, and now, after several years under their care, I can testify to the gratitude we feel for having made this good decision.[11]

Back to the metaphor of a quarterback, we have given these people complete access to all our financial decisions. Because of the wonder of technology, they have unfettered permission to look into our information, including banks where we have our

> THESE FOUR
> PROFESSIONALS—
> DOCTOR, ATTORNEY,
> ACCOUNTANT,
> FINANCIAL
> PLANNER—ARE LIKE
> YOUR PALLBEARERS.
> THEY MUST BE
> STRONG ENOUGH
> TO CARRY THE
> BOX AND SMART
> ENOUGH TO KNOW
> WHERE TO TAKE IT.

checking accounts. In addition to having quarterly meetings— virtually or in-person—these professionals have made themselves wonderfully available at a moment's notice.

While it may sound a little constricting, we don't make any significant purchases without a quick consultation with our financial planners. Thankfully, they're very responsive, so checking in with them is never a serious inconvenience.

These four professionals—doctor, attorney, accountant,

---

11. We found CapTrust in Holland, Michigan. Not only are Bruce Johnson and Kris Zylstra highly qualified, but their approach is gentle—patiently waiting for our nonfinancial brains to catch up—and precise. Visit their website at www .ctfa.com/the-captrust-team. You need to find a team like this one.

financial planner—are like your pallbearers.[12] They must be strong enough to carry the box and smart enough to know where to take it.

GETTING A ROUND TUIT

If you knew Zig Ziglar or ever attended one of his conferences, you've likely heard of the "round tuit." He had poker chips custom-made with the word *Tuit* stamped on them. Then he'd go into this hilarious riff about people who make goals and resolutions but just never follow through. "They never get around to it," he'd twang. "If that's you, here's a solution to your procrastination. A round tuit." And then he'd pass out those chips.

Some would laugh. Others would groan. Zig wasn't necessarily talking about end-of-life stuff but rather about just ordinary things we're temped to procrastinate about. All would understand because there's nothing weird or funny about this. If you don't have these four professionals—these pallbearers—in your life, time is not on your side. Before your funeral, these folks need to be identified and secured, and you need to turn them loose to straighten out your stuff. It's never too late to find the help you need.

At this point, you may be thinking to yourself, *I know all of this sounds right. And good. Someday soon I'll put together*

---

12. In the last chapter, I mentioned the need for a handyman for your house and a sexton for your place of worship—a go-to pastor who loves you. A pastor whom you love. I could add this person as a fifth pallbearer, but I'm going leave them back in the chapter where I've already talked about the need for them. Your pastor is strategic. These pallbearers are more tactical.

a plan. It shouldn't come as a surprise to learn that the Bible has something to say about procrastination. From the wisdom of James comes this: "If anyone, then, knows the good they ought to do and doesn't do it, it is sin for them" (4:17).

"Okay," I'm hoping you're saying. "I'm sold."

And as you'd guess, the real upside for securing these folks is not primarily for you. It's for the people you love who will outlive you. Each of these pallbearers—your personal pallbearers—will be a huge gift to them.

CAN I HELP?

This is a true story. A tough one to tell.

In January 2020, I sold my agency to my colleagues.

At that time, they had worked for me for a combined total of more than forty years. These men had invested their lives in building what Michael Hyatt and I started in 1992. Having them take the ownership reins was perfectly appropriate.

The month after the sale, I celebrated my seventy-second birthday. Even though these men were wildly gracious about my ongoing role in the company, I knew the years were taking their toll on me. In fact, within sixty days of the execution of the documents that sealed the sale, I was diagnosed with melanoma cancer. Two surgeries followed. A couple months after the second surgery, I was diagnosed with non-Hodgkin lymphoma, completely unrelated to the first cancer.

Needless to say, the year was dramatically interrupted by my inability to do my job. But my colleagues—now my bosses—were patient. And grace-filled about my absences.

The following year, once back in the saddle, I did my best to reengage at full strength. As you'd guess, I expressed my deep appreciation for what they had done to backfill on my behalf. However, catching up and getting back to absolute full strength was going to take time—if that would even be possible. One time on our daily video call, I thanked them for covering for me, even joking about the likelihood that, cancer or not, I was getting older and would occasionally miss a step. Or two.

I also confessed that if—no, when—it happened that I started "losing it," I would be the last to know. They would need to report this to me. They chuckled appropriately but knew I had spoken truth.

Fast-forward a few months. We're on the daily video call, and I was telling a story. One of my colleagues spoke: "You know you told us that story yesterday."

To say that I lost it would be an understatement. I was upset. Way out of character for me, I raised my voice, threatening to hit the "end" key on my computer and sign off on the call. (I don't ever remember doing this. Ever.) Their eyes widened. I could tell that these men whom I know so well, love seamlessly, and trust implicitly were shocked by my response. The call finished with only a few words spoken.

Coming to my senses right after we hung up,[13] I went back and asked their forgiveness. Thankfully and not surprisingly, grace was poured back.

But what had been done had been done. These guys did

---

13. Even though ending a call these days means pressing the end key on our phones, I guess we can still call it "hanging up"?

what I had quipped about. My forgetfulness was lost on me. And as predicted, I was the last to know.

I tell this story because it's your story. You are going to "lose it." One incremental step at a time, you're going to act your age. This will show up in the form of a blank mind. Your train of thought will get derailed in the middle of a sentence. You'll interrupt something you're saying with another unrelated thought, and try though you might, getting back to where you were is impossible. Names of familiar people will inexplicably vanish. A conversation you had last night will disappear from your screen. When someone asks where you had dinner last Saturday night . . . or yesterday . . . you'll find yourself stopping to think about it.

In fact, you'll pay special attention to ads that pop up everywhere—on television and online—for memory loss supplements and pills. Just for the record, if you feel like you're losing a step or two in the memory department, again, I encourage you to reach out to your doctor and ask about it. Sometimes advertisements for this stuff sounds too good to be true. Just mindless marketing. To help you comb through the noise, your physician is a great resource.

BACK TO THAT LAST WILL AND TESTAMENT . . . PUTTING IT IN WRITING

Two more things about your will. Let's call these a double encore.

Encore number one includes a remarkable woman. When I set out to write this book, as I've mentioned, I bought a bunch of books written by wiser, more experienced folks to help me. I read books like I write them—a sweet, long letter to one person; a deep conversation across a cup of coffee.

One of the friends I met during the research phase of writing was Katie—actually, Kathryn Butler, MD. My agency has the privilege of helping this remarkable talent find publishers for her writing.

One book that had a great deal of impact on my thinking during this process was her *Between Life and Death*.[14] As the doctor on call, Katie tells many end-of-life stories in this book. You'll find these helpful, as I did, to unwrap the unique challenges of choices when a person's life is fast approaching the finish line.

The book includes Dr. Butler's own sample advance directive. As something of a disclaimer, she writes, "I offer the following as an example. When you formulate your own advance directive, I urge you to consider your unique medical history and the facets of life pivotal to your walk of faith."[15]

Here are a few sentences to give you an idea of what Katie has written for her own survivors:

> In the event that severe illness incapacitates me, I wish for my [chief surrogate] to direct decisions in my medical care on my behalf. Should catastrophic also incapacitate him, this responsibility should fall to [secondary surrogate].
>
> As a follower of Jesus Christ, I aim to preserve

14. Kathryn Butler, *Between Life and Death: A Gospel-Centered Guide to End-of-Life Medical Care* (Wheaton, IL: Crossway, 2019). You can read about Katie at all sorts of places on the internet. Simply google "Dr. Kathryn Butler" and you'll find some very helpful stuff on her life and work.
15. Butler, *Between Life and Death*, 185.

God-given life when feasible but not to ignore his authority over the extent of my life or to chase after treatments that would thwart my ability to faithfully serve him. In general, I will pursue treatments that promise recovery but not those that prolong death or those that permanently eliminate my abilities to reason and communicate.[16]

How good is this?

Now, we had an attorney of our very own with whom Nancy and I were able to discuss in great detail all the twists and turns of what needed to be included. I commend to you having a conversation like this one with a professional you trust.

And now with the legal and more technical issues behind us, there's something fun I'd like to tease out for your finish line to-do list.

---

16. Butler, *Between Life and Death*, 185 (see 185–88 for her complete advance directive).

SEVEN

SAYING GRACE

Be blessed and be a blessing.

NANCY DEMOSS WOLGEMUTH[1]

Gesundheit![2] A few months ago, I was riding the Skylink shuttle located in the fifty-first state in our union, also known as the DFW airport. Go ahead and google "gargantuan assembly," and you'll get a photo of this amazing place. As our little train rocketed from terminal to terminal, I was standing, hanging on to the handrail to avoid winding up in the lap of an older guy sitting nearby. Presently I got a little tickle in my nose and sneezed. This was during COVID-19, so I was

---

1. Nancy says this to nearly everyone leaving our house. She's done this for many years.
2. In German, *Gesundheit* means "health" (and "sanity"). Wishing "good health" was once thought to hold off the illness that might follow a sneeze.

wearing a mask, thus no contagious, diseased snot droplets were sent airborne.

A total stranger who was standing close by said, "God bless you."[3]

I nodded and audibly thanked him.

Isn't it interesting that this holy expression is as popular as Chick-fil-A and suitcases with wheels? At least, I find it fascinating.

In fact, the fellow traveler was revealing something we read about in the first book of the Bible—blessing.

START AT THE
VERY BEGINNING

Let's turn the clock back. Not just to earlier today or last week or a year ago or even back to when you were born. Turn it back to the beginning of time, even before there was such a thing as time.

In the beginning God created the heavens and the earth. Now the earth was formless and empty, darkness was over the surface of the deep, and the Spirit of God was hovering over the waters. (Genesis 1:1–2)

This is a moment that's hard to consider. Our wildest imaginations simply don't engage here. The words *formless* and *empty* and *darkness* paint a picture we cannot

---

3. When Nancy or I sneeze, we say, "I love you." We've told many people about this, and around here it's catching on.

comprehend. This isn't just a starless night or a pitch-dark room; this is a universe of nothingness. Stop and try to consider this. It's not easy, is it?

And then, right here, right now, we are introduced to God. First, there's a vacuum. Congenital emptiness. And then there is something. No, actually, not some*thing*. Some*One*. God, who was there all along.

And this God begins to speak. And what does He say? He creates. He makes things using only His voice. He creates every single thing. He doesn't even use His hands. He only speaks.

As you probably know, the next few days included the creation of daylight, land mass and sea, and all kinds of vegetation.

After that, God says . . .

"Let the water teem with living creatures, and let birds fly above the earth across the vault of the sky." So God created the great creatures of the sea and every living thing with which the water teems and that moves about in it, according to their kinds, and every winged bird according to its kind. And God saw that it was good. God blessed them. (Genesis 1:20–22)

God creates fish and birds, and then He blesses them. There it is. That word the guy used on the airport tram— *bless*. This is the first time we see *bless* in the Bible, and God uses it as an affirmation of what He had just done. In fact, He says to the birds and the fish, "Bless you. Have at it,

kids. Enjoy." That's right, He invites them to have babies.[4]
Procreation follows His blessing.

Living, as Nancy and I do, just a few miles from Lake
Michigan, we've seen firsthand something about the fish that
fill this huge "freshwater ocean." Actually, a few years ago,
my colleagues and I made a serious catch of fish and lifted
some of those bad boys onto the deck of our rented boat.

And almost every day, I get to see a bald eagle—or two—
fly by and sometimes swoop down to catch lunch from the
St. Joseph River, just behind our home. At this moment,
I'm watching more than forty wild swans lazily swimming
upstream in the frigid river.

Fish and birds are blessed by God. How cool is that?
And remember that the creation of these things happened
with the sound of God's voice. That was all. His voice.

Okay, we have creation—the universe, the earth, seas and
dry land, plants, birds, fish, animals. But there's more.

> Then God said, "Let us make mankind in our image, in
> our likeness, so that they may rule over the fish in the
> sea and the birds in the sky, over the livestock and all the
> wild animals, and over all the creatures that move along
> the ground."

> So God created mankind in his own image,
>   in the image of God he created them;
>   male and female he created them.

---

4. Or in this case, lay plenty of eggs.

God blessed them and said to them, "Be fruitful and increase in number; fill the earth and subdue it. Rule over the fish in the sea and the birds in the sky and over every living creature that moves on the ground." (1:26–28)

Finally, in this unimaginable odyssey, God creates man and woman. And He blesses them too. And on the heels of that blessing, like the fish and the birds, He tells them to have babies. It's like our heavenly Father knew that His blessing needed to move from Him to us and from us to our children and grandchildren. "God created mankind in his own image, in the image of God he created them; male and female he created them. God blessed them and said to them, 'Be fruitful and increase in number; fill the earth and subdue it'" (1:27–28).

There it is again. Procreation follows His blessing. (Do I hear an "amen?")

Here, for the first time in recorded history we're introduced to the idea of blessing. *The* blessing. God's blessing over people . . . us . . . you and me.

As the commentator James McKeown says, "The importance of the theme of blessing lies in its significance as an indicator of a person's relationship with God."[5]

We know what a blessing is, like saying "grace" for our meals, but what exactly is *the* blessing? And why does the Old Testament make such a big deal about it? And at our stage of life, is there something we should be doing about it?

---

5. Quoted in Paul Barker, "Blessing in the Old Testament: A Biblical Theology of Blessing (2)," Gospel Coalition Australia, December 5, 2015, https://au.thegospelcoalition.org/article/blessing-in-the-old-testament-a-biblical-theology-of-blessing-2.

Let me begin with an answer to the last question. Yes, there *is* something to "blessing," and I'm hoping that shortly you'll also embrace the idea for yourself.

GRAYBILL

My paternal grandfather was Graybill Graybill Wolgemuth. Yes, I'm serious. His name was Graybill Graybill Wolgemuth. A third-generation Swiss-German immigrant, this man was the most mysterious creature I knew as a young boy. He was also morbidly serious. All the time.

In 1991, Graybill's son, my dad, asked me to visit his father, who wasn't far from the literal gates of Heaven. I sat on the edge of my grandfather's small single bed in their Lancaster County home. It was one of the first times I had seen him smile. I mean, really smile. He recognized me and took me by the hand. We made small talk for a few minutes—my voyage to Pennsylvania, the weather—and then he lifted his hand, white, luminous skin stretched tight over the bones, and placed it on my shoulder. Looking me squarely in the eye, he smiled even broader and prayed.

"Thank you, Lord, for Robert," he prayed. "Today I bless him."

Even though I was in my forties, in that moment I felt like a much younger man, and this was wonderful. My throat tightened and my eyes brimmed with tears. The best I can describe it is that it was a holy moment. And I believe he meant those words as a blessing, transferred from an aged man to his grandson.

Graybill had been a self-educated student of the Bible and a bivocational pastor-farmer his entire adult life. He knew well the biblical tradition of blessings, such as the account of Jacob blessing his son Joseph and his grandsons Manasseh and Ephraim.

This story is found in chapter 48 of the Old Testament book of Genesis. If you grew up in the church, you likely heard pieces and parts of this story. If not, it's worth repeating. But before I do, let me take a minute to tell you about the whole idea of "blessing."

As we travel through the pages of the Old Testament, we find examples of blessing. God blesses people, and people bless other people. We see this in the blessing on Noah (Genesis 6:22; 8:20–9:17), in the greetings of Boaz (Ruth 2:4, 12), and especially in the Aaronic blessing: "The LORD bless you and keep you; the LORD make his face shine on you and be gracious to you; the LORD turn his face toward you and give you peace" (Numbers 6:24–26).

And when you take a close look at examples of this blessing, it's clear that God does not dispense holy blessings haphazardly. He doesn't throw them out like clowns in a parade tossing candy to little kids sitting on the curb. No, God purposefully bestows His blessing on those who are in harmony with Him.

If I may, as promised, a quick detour to a graphic blessing scene in the Old Testament. Jacob—also known as Israel— was a very old man. Nearing his finish line. The full account of his life is a Hollywood movie script if there ever was one. Unable to see, the feeble patriarch calls for his son Joseph and his two grandsons Ephraim and Manasseh. Jacob gathers them onto his lap and speaks. Joseph bows low before his dying father. What a gentle scene.

Then [Jacob] blessed Joseph and said,

"May the God before whom my fathers
    Abraham and Isaac walked faithfully,
the God who has been my shepherd
    all my life to this day,
the Angel who has delivered me from
    all harm—
may he bless these boys.
May they be called by my name
    and the names of my fathers Abraham
        and Isaac,
and may they increase greatly on the earth."
(Genesis 48:15–16)

An old man gathering his son and grandsons and pronouncing a blessing. What an incredible picture. And this is a picture of what you and I might be inspired to do.

THE ODDS ARE IN YOUR FAVOR

The chances that you will die suddenly, with no warning, are less than 50 percent. Much less. You're walking down the street or on the golf course or having lunch with a friend, and you die. Bam! One moment you're chatting away, and next moment you're not breathing.

Even though it could, this will most likely not happen to you. The odds are in your favor that you'll have a chance to speak before you die. So while you are able, what would you like to say? Whom do you need to bless?

Like "saying grace" before a meal, asking God to miraculously turn lifeless food into something special, there are people in your life who need to hear a blessing. From you. While you're still alive. And because of your age and standing in your family, you have the currency to do this.

Your chances for a sudden death are actually only about 7 percent. Ninety three percent of the men and women you know will have a chance to pronounce a blessing before they die. But 100 percent of us—you and me—are alive at this moment. A decision to bless our mate, our children, and grandchildren before we cross our own finish line can still be done, and it's a really good idea.

Back in 1986, the company I worked for published a book with a title and subtitle that needed no explanation: *The Blessing: Giving the Gift of Unconditional Love and Acceptance*.[6] My friends Dr. John Trent and the late Gary Smalley teamed up to craft a perennial bestseller that has sold more than a million copies.

---

6. John Trent and Gary Smalley, *The Blessing: Giving the Gift of Unconditional Love and Acceptance*, rev. ed. (1986; repr., Nashville: W Publishing, 2019). The latest edition of this book was coauthored with Kari Trent Stageberg, John's oldest daughter and a gifted writer. I commend this excellent resource to you.

Dr. Trent's participation in the writing of this book came out of the crucible of his own tragic experience:

> I sat with my father for eight and a half hours in a small hospice room on the day he died. He was dying of congestive heart and lung failure—a terrible way to die. I held his hand during the tough, horrible coughing parts. I told him I loved him. I got him water. I tried to help him get comfortable as much as I could. I prayed for him—and had him cuss at me for praying for him.[7]

Not long ago, John and I spoke about this hard moment in his life and the importance of speaking—or writing—blessings for your mate, your children, and your grandchildren. He left no room for uncertainty. It's your responsibility and privilege to bless them.

For many decades, John has given his life to helping ordinary folks like you and me. People with children and grandchildren. His strategy is to give us specific tools to pass along a blessing. He does this tenderly. Brilliantly.[8]

You and I are discussing things we ought to be doing during these sunset years. We're likely the matriarchs or patriarchs of our families. Simply because of our age and the color of our hair we have earned the right—the platform—to hold court. To speak with authority. I've watched with deep interest John's presentation of the blessing. To say I highly

---

7. Trent, Smalley, and Stageberg, *The Blessing*, 8.
8. For example, see "The Blessing Day," Legacy Minded Men, accessed June 15, 2022, www.legacymindedmen.org/the-blessing-day.

recommend his video to you will be one of the glaring understatements of this book. You will thank me.

But there's a lot more to warranting this blessing privilege than sporting myriad candles on our birthday cakes. It's actually good for us.

At our age, you and I attend more funerals than weddings. Nancy and I have been to so many since we married in 2015 that we've lost count. But King Solomon was surely onto something when he wrote, "It is better to go to a house of mourning than to go to a house of feasting, for death is the destiny of everyone; the living should take this to heart" (Ecclesiastes 7:2).

There it is. "The living." That's you and me.

During the months I was writing the manuscript for this book, we attended three funerals of men in their eighties and nineties. We knew these saints. Very well. And what Nancy and I talked about as we drove away from the venues that hosted their services was the vigorous demonstration of their love for God. No one had any doubts about the discipline they exhibited in spending alone time in His Word and telling others of their devotion to the Lord Jesus.

Oh, and they loved their families. The tributes from children and grandchildren sent chills down everyone's collective backs.

So with the days (weeks, months, years) I have left, I further resolved to bless my family with words and touches—and to do so from a heart that is first humble before God.

If you had been alive during the times of the writing of the Old Testament, you would be more than familiar with the word—and the concept of—*blessing*. On its website, the

Fellowship of Israel Related Ministries (FIRM) reminds us that almost every formal Jewish prayer starts with the words *Baruch Ata Adonai.* "Blessed are You, our Lord." The post goes on to say:

> For an idea this common, it's astounding how the true power of it has been overlooked. Because to bless and be blessed is a fundamental part of our relationship with God, as well as relationships with other people. Blessings, whether given or received, help us recognize God in our lives and draw closer to Him. It is not a recognition of riches, rather a humble confession that we are not self-sufficient.[9]

TAKE THEM TO YOUR FATHER FIRST

Speaking a blessing to your progeny or to other younger people may feel a little—or maybe a lot—awkward. You may be wondering about the setting of such a conversation, not to mention some anxiety over what you should say.

I have an idea. In the words of Pat Riley, the legendary NBA coach, "Practice, practice, practice." But it's not what you think. You're not actually sitting your children down and having a blessing dress rehearsal. No, what you're doing to get your heart ready to give a blessing can be done in prayer.

Every night before Nancy and I go off to sleep, we cuddle

---

9. See Estera Wieja, "Blessed in Hebrew: The Meaning behind the Word Baruch," Fellowship of Israel Related Ministries, April 30, 2020, https://firmisrael.org/learn/the-hebrew-meaning-of-blessed.

and I pray. First, I thank the Lord for who He is. His creation, His love, His care, His sovereignty over everything, including the day we have just finished. I thank Him for each event, each conversation, each decision.

Then I go down a list of folks He has prompted me to love, pray for, and bless. By name I ask Him to reveal Himself to and bless Nancy, my children, my grandchildren, my great-grandson, Nancy's mother, and her family. Then there's a list of a dozen or so young men and women for whom we've been asked to pray. These are sons and daughters of good friends who have for specific reasons asked us to pray for their children.[10]

We ask the Father to speak, to protect, and to *bless* these young people. Some are prodigals, a few are in the process of making life-altering decisions, and still others are predictably facing the temptations common to you and me.

I mention this habit not to brag, only to give you an idea of how I have experienced the joy and privilege of blessing younger people in my life. This is a habit that can be verbalized day after day. Speaking their names gives me a picture of who I'm praying for. And even though most of these people are grown, I envision actually lifting their bodies toward Heaven, like a biblical priest would do when blessing a child.

Every once in a while, Nancy and I have the chance to bless the parents of these individuals by telling them we pray for their son or daughter every day by name. And even though

---

10. Our dear friend Paul Johnson stepped into Heaven in 2021 at the age of ninety-three. At his service, one of the speakers told us that Paul and his wife Pam prayed for 150 people by name every night. I have double-checked this. It's true.

these parents thank us—and that is gratifying, for sure—it's not the primary reason we pray for their offspring. We do this because we've promised someone we would do it, and we believe that God hears our prayers and, by His grace, goes out of His way to look after these young men and women.

> GOD KNOWS MY HEART, AND HE HAS TOLD US TO BRING OUR PETITIONS TO HIM. IN OBEDIENCE, I'M DOING JUST THAT. HIS PROMISE WHEN I PRAY IS TO LISTEN AND ANSWER. AND BLESS.

But does my prayer—or my blessing—for these young people every day actually make a difference? Does God say in response to my prayer, "Actually, I wasn't paying much attention to that guy you just prayed for—or prayed a blessing over—but since you've mentioned it, let Me see if I can spare a few minutes to help out."

Silly, right? No.

God knows my heart, and He has told us to bring our petitions to Him. In obedience, I'm doing just that. His promise when I pray is to listen and answer. And bless.

BLESSING MY GRANDS

As of this writing, I have five grandchildren. Actually, given the ages of my daughters, I'm confident that this number is secure.

However, the number of my great-grands is currently at one and will surely climb, maybe before but certainly after I'm gone.

121

So since the number of my grandchildren is a fixed number, the following paragraphs are my blessing for them. If you can borrow these as a model for your children or grandchildren, I'd be honored. Help yourself.

ABIGAIL GRACE SCHRADER QUIRIN

You are my first grandchild, born on February 1, 1996. I was only forty-eight years old. Bobbie was forty-six. Young to be grandparents, to be sure. So we had a chance to sort of grow up with you. Very early on, Bobbie recognized that you had a sweet singing voice. She spent many hours teaching you many great hymns of our faith.

I bless you, Abby, not only because of your smile, your genuine love for people, or your lovely singing voice, but because of your precious heart. Your love for Jesus and His Word is front and center as you love Ben and raise your son, Ezra Dean, to be a man of God.

> Sing to the LORD a new song;
>   sing to the LORD, all the earth. (Psalm 96:1)

LUKE DAVID SCHRADER

You were my first grandson. Because of a building project I helped to shepherd at your dad and mom's house when you were a youngster, you and I made multiple trips to Home Depot. On those drives, we talked. Your gentle and winsome spirit drew me in. Yes, I was your granddaddy, but it was clear during those years, and the many that followed, that I was also your friend.

Now you are a grown and deeply thoughtful man, and you and I continue to talk. From your car. Thanks to FaceTime, you and I regularly catch up on each other's lives. Your winsome smile and upbeat attitude about life are contagious, the reason you are surrounded by many friends who love you. You love Christ, and you've made church a non-negotiable priority. This commitment will shape you for the remainder of your life as no other thing will. I bless you, Luke, with my "life verse."

> The LORD is my light and my salvation—
>   whom shall I fear?
> The LORD is the stronghold of my life—
>   of whom shall I be afraid?
> (Psalm 27:1)

ISAAC THOMAS SCHRADER

You are my second grandson and our family's gentle giant. You have been your own man from day one. Daring to climb an unclimbable tree right in front of us all or wearing your complete, brand-new outdoor camping gear to the table at Christmas dinner. Though sometimes subtle, your humor often inspires our family to sidesplitting decibels. No wonder Missy and Jon gave you a name that means "he will laugh, he will rejoice."

Though you generally dodge the limelight, your deep and godly character is worthy of a place of leadership that I believe God has in store for you. I bless you with words spoken by the apostle Paul about the way of Jesus:

Do nothing out of selfish ambition or vain conceit. Rather, in humility value others above yourselves, not looking to your own interests but each of you to the interests of the others. (Philippians 2:3–4)

HARPER CORIN TASSY
Julie and Christopher's firstborn is next. This young woman takes the expression "strong-willed child" to the next level. A gift from her mother, to be sure, right along with an entrepreneurial bent.

Like Isaac, you are your own person, Harper, and also like Isaac, not defiant or rude. Gentle and kind, you face life with certainty and focus.

You are a leader. A trendsetter. A person others emulate, thus a person who willingly goes first. I bless you.

Although he hadn't met you when he wrote this, King Solomon could have had you in mind when he penned these words:

> Trust in the LORD with all your heart
>> and lean not on your own understanding;
> in all your ways submit to him,
>> and he will make your paths straight.
> (Proverbs 3:5–6)

Last, but in no way least, is:

ELLA PATRICE TASSY
. . . aka Ella Bean. I start this blessing with a Bible verse that might as well have your name on it:

> Be kind and compassionate to one another, forgiving each
> other, just as in Christ God forgave you. (Ephesians 4:32)

Your tenderness has been your trademark from the beginning. Does this mean you're a wimp? Do you lack courage? Absolutely not. (Be on the business end of a volleyball spike and you'll find out.) But your genuine love for people has bound you to so many, especially your family. Your patience and humility will always be fastened to your life, your way will always be the way of peace.

If God blesses you with marriage and children someday, they will see everyone as a mission field, a place to love and minister to all, including "the least of these," just like your mother does. I bless you with a second verse:

> Be completely humble and gentle; be patient, bearing with
> one another in love. Make every effort to keep the unity
> of the Spirit through the bond of peace. (Ephesians 4:2–3)

◆ ◆ ◆

As the blesser, the one issuing these blessings, my faith must be in Christ. His life, death, and resurrection must be my resting place. My life has to point to this and not to me. When I choose to bless others, I am turning them over to Jesus. Self-sufficiency or self-promotion isn't going to cut it.

Back to our blessing prayer before Nancy and I nod off to sleep, our own hearts must be clean—forgiven—so as not to ask for God to do His work in them with the wrong motives. It must come from humble hearts of sincere love. A love that survives testing . . . this kind of testing.

THE WAITING FATHER AND THE ELDER BROTHER

One of the best-known Bible stories of all time is the account of the prodigal son. Many years ago, my understanding of this story was turned on its head. Two men I deeply respect were responsible for this upending.

First, because my firm represented the book-writing of John MacArthur, the publisher asked me to accompany John on a tour of eight major markets. The plan was to find large churches that would host him as a speaker on the subject, helping to promote his book *The Tale of Two Sons*.[11]

To say that traveling for a couple weeks with John was delightful doesn't come close to describing it. The arrangements and financial details of the voyage around the country were covered by the publisher. The speaking was John's charge. And I was to help host the church meetings, lead the congregation in singing a hymn or two, shepherd the book signings afterward, and be John's traveling companion. Sounds like fun, doesn't it? It was.

Hearing the same message eight times in two weeks left an indelible mark on me. Let me cut to the chase. For years, the story found in Luke 15, has been called "the Prodigal

---

11. John MacArthur, *A Tale of Two Sons: The Inside Story of a Father, His Sons, and a Shocking Murder* (Nashville: Nelson, 2008).

Son." That's inaccurate titling. It should be called "the Waiting Father."

I'm sure the tale is familiar to you. But the book—and John's message—was focused on the prodigal's dad. In unpacking a breathtaking story for His spellbound audience of religious people Jesus was painting a picture. Of Himself. The father who not just received his sinful boy home, but actually had forgiven him before the son ever decided to return.

And when the son did find his way home, the father ran—literally ran, an extremely uncool thing for a man of means back in that day—to meet him. To embrace his filthy frame. To bless him.

What about the other son?

In the late 1980s, I had the joy of hosting Dr. Tim Keller at a gathering I helped to lead called the Foundation Conference. This three-day affair was populated with "veteran Christians"—people like me who had been Christ followers for many years.

Perfect for this particular group, Tim's message that day highlighted the "elder brother." He spoke of the two besetting sins that plague every man and woman: unrighteousness and self-righteousness. I cannot remember feeling more like a speaker was looking at me, even though I was behind him on the platform.

More than just talking about naughty boys who run away from home, Jesus was talking about respectable sinners. Again, just like me. Because of a self-righteous attitude, this son never had a chance to celebrate his father's blessing.

Why am I taking valuable time here to review this story? What does this have to do with the blessing? Here it is: whether you and I connect viscerally with the rebellious younger brother or the arrogant elder brother, we have a Father who is eager not only to forgive but to embrace us, to call us, to bless us, and to give us the authority to bless others. This is truth.

WHEN THE BLESSING IS A THING

One of the biblical accounts of blessing is found in Genesis 27. For many, this is a troublesome story because it involves deception and flat-out lying. But it seems like the Bible ignores this and the blessing goes out anyway.

Okay, I'm getting a little ahead of myself.

I'm talking about one of the patriarchs of God's chosen people, Isaac. A very old man.[12]

Esau and Jacob were Isaac's sons. The former was a man's man. A hunter—an outdoors guy—and covered head to toe with thick hair. The latter, Jacob, never needed to apply sunscreen. He spent most of his days inside reading recipe books and conspiring with the parent who loved him more—his mother, Rebekah. Google "dysfunctional family," and a picture of these four will pop up on your screen.

You're welcome to read the story for yourself, but Jacob—with the encouragement of his mother—deceived his dim-eyed father into giving the blessing traditionally reserved for the firstborn Esau to Jacob instead.

---

12. Isaac was 180 years old when he died. This portion of his story happened near the end of his life.

Thinking he was blessing Esau, Isaac spoke these words to the rascal Jacob:

> "May God give you heaven's dew and earth's
> richness—
> an abundance of grain and new wine.
> May nations serve you
> and peoples bow down to you.
> Be lord over your brothers,
> and may the sons of your mother bow
> down to you.
> May those who curse you be cursed
> and those who bless you be blessed"
> (Genesis 27:28–29).

Soon, Jacob left his father's presence, and then Esau—the real Esau—returned, greeting his father. Once Isaac realized he had been tricked into blessing the wrong son, Scripture says that "he trembled violently" (Genesis 27:33). Then Esau begged his father to bless him too. But Isaac wailed, "Your brother came deceitfully and took your blessing" (v. 35).

It was like Isaac's blessing was an actual physical gift. A treasure he could only give once. Under a cruel deception, the father gave the blessing to the wrong son, and he could not give it again. How could this be?

It's true that Jacob swiped his father's blessing from his big brother, Esau, but it's also true that Esau "despised" his birthright (Genesis 25:34). Long before Jacob deceived their aging father into granting him the blessing, Esau chose foolishness by openly rejecting his birthright. Centuries later, the apostle Paul nails this for us: "Do not be deceived: God cannot be mocked. A man reaps what he sows" (Galatians 6:7).

This is true for both Jacob and Esau. After overhearing his brother's rage when he discovers his little brother's treachery, Jacob ran for fear of his life, living in exile for many years. And it seems like the years of regret—and taking some of his own medicine from Uncle Laban—taught Jacob something about the "wages" of the sin against his brother.[13]

One of my favorite Bible stories recounts the first meeting of these two men, at least two decades after the "give me your blessing" gambit. For good reason, Jacob was paralyzed with fear. His big—and much stronger—warrior brother should have crushed him for his deceit. But as it turned out, their father's blessing was like a seed planted in Jacob's heart. And Esau had clearly come to terms with his own culpability in the matter as well. Although their father had been dead for a long time, surely he would have been thrilled with the outcome of his sons' first meeting: "But Esau ran to meet Jacob and embraced him; he threw his arms around his neck and kissed him. And they wept" (Genesis 33:4).

For you and me, the lesson is that as blessing givers, we are showing our progeny the power and the joy of receiving this blessing ourselves and living the same truth when it's our turn. It's as though Jacob and Esau were confessing to each other, "Even though he's dead and gone, our humble father

---

13. You can read in Genesis 28–31 about Jacob's life during the years after he cheated his brother out of the blessing. In God's providence, Jacob is forced to deal with Uncle Laban, a man who was the kind of chiseler he was. Apparently a lesson was learned.

showed us how to do this blessing thing. Now we can learn to do the same."

My old friend and college classmate Dr. Hal Habecker founded a vibrant ministry several years ago called "Finishing Well." This quote is from a helpful book he wrote called *What the Bible Says about Growing Older.* I enthusiastically commend Hal's wisdom and this ministry to you: "The Scriptures teach us that aging people have a mission in life with respect to future generations—to keep challenging and encouraging the generations behind us to continue following our example of trusting the power of God in our lives."[14]

> AS BLESSING GIVERS, WE ARE SHOWING OUR PROGENY THE POWER AND THE JOY OF RECEIVING THIS BLESSING OURSELVES AND LIVING THE SAME TRUTH WHEN IT'S OUR TURN.

This is why you and I bless our children. It's a privilege to "say grace" over them. Not so they say nice things about us at our funerals, but that they learn from our example to bless—say grace over—others.[15]

We bless them so they know they are loved and handed to God. We bless them so they live in the grace and confidence of God's work in them. We bless them to give them a head start in making their faith in Christ their own. We bless them, asking that their ears and hearts be attuned to the

---

14. Hal Habecker, *What the Bible Says about Growing Older: The Exciting Potential in This Season of Life* (Plano, TX: Finishing Well Ministries, 2022), 30.
15. On the very day I wrote this, I had a chance to FaceTime with my five-day-old great-grandson, Ezra Dean Quirin. His parents, granddaughter Abby, and her husband Ben helped with the technology. At the close of our conversation, I prayed a blessing over this tiny little boy. And his parents and Nancy joined in. It was pure joy.

Savior's voice, knowing that the work and power of God's Holy Spirit can alert and challenge them to lead lives of obedience and kingdom service.

You know, bless it forward.

Before you and I cross the finish line.

EIGHT

WHO WILL BE YOUR PALLBEARERS?

Death is the one time when everybody becomes a somebody.

Philip Yancey, *Where the Light Fell*

Funerals can be excellent conversation starters. Especially with your mate.

During the summer of 2015, Nancy and I were visiting my daughter Julie and her husband, Christopher, in Charlotte. We were engaged but not married. Nancy stayed in my second home there. I slept at Julie and Christopher's just a few miles away.

Early one morning, I drove back to the house to make coffee. Nancy was still resting upstairs. In an hour or so, she stepped onto the back patio and greeted me. As she wiped the sleep from her eyes, I could tell there was more. It wasn't just sleep; it was tears.

"Elisabeth Elliot just passed away," Nancy said. "I just received a text from a close friend telling me the news."

I quickly stood and walked over to her. As I held her close, the only sounds were Nancy's muffled sobs.

When she had gathered her composure, she filled me in on the sad details.

As you may know, Elisabeth Elliot was a beloved author and speaker. The wife of the late Jim Elliot, a missionary who had been martyred in Ecuador in 1956. For sixty years, Elisabeth had capably carried her late husband's mantle, returning to Ecuador with her young daughter for several years to love and minister to the same people who had speared her husband to death on the riverbank.

In addition to traveling around the world, speaking, and writing, Elisabeth had also started a daily fifteen-minute radio program called Gateway to Joy. And after thirteen years, the baton was handed to Nancy.

On Friday, August 31, 2001, Elisabeth opened with her beloved and familiar, "You are loved with an everlasting love, that's what the Bible says, and underneath are the everlasting arms. This is your friend Elisabeth Elliot."

That soft, deep voice would then proceed to tell her listeners what she would be talking about that day.

On Monday, September 3, the very next week, on more than three hundred radio stations, Nancy welcomed Gateway to Joy's listeners to a new, replacement broadcast called Revive Our Hearts—her own radio ministry.

So the ministry relationship between Elisabeth and Nancy had been established.

And now on that warm June morning on my patio, Nancy was really feeling the weight of the death of a woman whose impact on her had been profound.

A few weeks later, the first of two funerals was held for Elisabeth in Boston. We were there to celebrate the life and the faithful ministry of this remarkable woman. We arrived early at the chapel on the campus of Gordon College and Seminary. Elisabeth's open casket was resting in front at the altar.

Nancy and I walked, hand in hand, down the center aisle to pay our last respects. As we approached, I was struck by the humble appearance of the casket, which was made of unpainted, exterior half-inch plywood with one-by-twos stapled inside at the seams. Even during my construction days, I had never seen a more spartan crate, even on job sites. The interior of the coffer had a simple, narrow sheet on which Elisabeth's body was lying. No tufts of satin fabric. Or pillow. Just an ordinary slice of unbleached muslin. I did my best to mask my surprise at this crude display.

Nancy and I waited until we were driving away from the cemetery several hours later to talk about the casket.

"I love the simplicity of Elisabeth's casket," Nancy said. "I'd like to have something similar when I die."

"You would?" I responded, unable to camouflage my surprise.

Going into detail and unpacking the rest of this

conversation, which included what I'd like to have for my own casket, is something I'll not disclose here. But suffice it to say, this was a talk that needed to happen.

You need to have the same conversation with your mate and loved ones. Some people really care about this particular detail of their death strategy.

Some don't.[1]

CREMATION

If you want to initiate a lively conversation among your friends, bring up the topic of cremation.

Some eager environmentalists will quickly jump in, describing the footprint difference between a casket vault and an urn. In fact, some people not only don't bury the thing that contains the ashes of their loved ones, but they bring it home for the fireplace mantel or take the container for a ride and scatter the ashes somewhere meaningful in memory of the dead person.

Many of my friends, whose wisdom, knowledge of the Scriptures, and love for Christ I deeply admire, have differing opinions about this issue. In fact, Pastor Alistair Begg[2] has some interesting things to say about what we choose to

---

1. Along with the other details of your funeral, you may want to clarify your wishes to your mate while you can. When you look into this, you'll discover that funeral homes typically bundle all their services in one, including the cost of the casket, which ranges in cost from the spartan kind that Elisabeth Elliot used to very expensive ornate ones.

2. For many years the pastor of Parkside Church in the Cleveland area, Alistair kindly agreed to speak at Bobbie's funeral.

do with our corpses. I commend Alistair's helpful conversation about this to you.[3]

THE PLOT THICKENS

Because I will likely expire in Michigan, I wanted to ask my daughters if it would be okay for me to buried there, even though their mother's body lies quietly in the state of Florida. Since their mother died in 2014 and their dad moved to Michigan in 2015, did they still want us to be buried in the same cemetery, or would it be okay if I were to choose two spaces in the ground for Nancy and me, finding plots near our home in the Great Lakes State?

You may think this isn't that big a deal, but when I asked them, I could tell that the request stung. Even if just a little. If they say yes to the request, this means their parents' bodies will be buried 1,128 miles apart. They knew that when Bobbie and I moved to Orlando, we checked out a cemetery less than a half mile from the home we purchased. But, now, more than twenty years later, I'm talking with them about Nancy and me both being interred in Michigan. They graciously agreed that would be fine.

Nancy and I plan to be buried in a cemetery near our home, in a small town called Buchanan.

Although Nancy had visited the place many times before, my first visit was in 2015 when we were courting. We went there so she could show me the headstone of a dear friend,

---

3. Alistair Begg, "On Death and Dying," Truth for Life, July 22, 2007, www
.truthforlife.org/resources/sermon/on-death-and-dying.

Del Fehsenfeld, Jr., whom I mentioned in chapter 3. This special man was the founder of Life Action Ministries, and in 1980 he invited Nancy to become a part of what God was already doing through this outreach. With some prayer and seeking the advice of godly friends, Nancy said yes.

Then nine years later, in 1989, only seven months after the initial diagnosis, Del died of a brain tumor. He was forty-two. And his death was a terrific blow to Nancy. Her ministry mentor and friend was gone. Even as a person with huge confidence in a sovereign God, she had a hard time putting it all together. As you can imagine, the "why?" questions were relentless.

So Del was buried in a Michigan cemetery. We stood in front of his marble headstone, where Nancy read aloud these words:

Del Fehsenfeld, Jr. 1947–1989

Founder, Life Action Ministries
He Knew God
He Loved God
He Walked with God
He Believed God
He Lived and Died for the Glory of God
2 Chronicles 16:9 [4]

Nancy and I have had the joy of hosting Del's family in our home. Many times. His children and grandchildren

---

4. "For the eyes of the LORD range throughout the earth to strengthen those whose hearts are fully committed to him."

speak of this man with deepest admiration, respect, joy, and love. There is always plenty of affection and laughter. We have gathered around our piano, with Del's widow's husband, Rev. Robert (Bob) Parks, a widower himself, at the keyboard. "Great Is Thy Faithfulness" has been sung with huge smiles—and a tear or two—on each face.

Pardon for sin and a peace that endureth,
Thine own dear presence to cheer and to guide,
Strength for today and bright hope for tomorrow,
Blessings all mine, with ten thousand beside! [5]

THE FUNERAL . . . YOUR FUNERAL

A small, family funeral service for Del was held in a beautiful little chapel, barely 500 yards from our home in Michigan, followed days later by a larger, public memorial service in a nearby church.

One day, long after you're gone, your children and close friends will remember your funeral. What will they recall feeling? Or thinking? Or saying? Or singing?

This may feel strange, but may I suggest that you go ahead and plan for this event? Soon.

Several years ago, I made this outline. It sits right here in my computer, filed under "Personal" and "RDW Memorial Service."

Occasionally updating this file, I have identified the

---

5. Thomas O. Chisholm, "Great Is Thy Faithfulness" (1923). Public domain.

pastor I've already asked to shepherd the service. Those who will speak have already said yes. The hymns I'd like sung are also chosen and included in this document.

> ONE DAY, LONG AFTER YOU'RE GONE, YOUR CHILDREN AND CLOSE FRIENDS WILL REMEMBER YOUR FUNERAL. WHAT WILL THEY RECALL FEELING? OR THINKING? OR SAYING? OR SINGING?

The burial plot I've picked out, as I mentioned, is in Buchanan, Michigan, actually not far from Del Fehsenfeld's plot.

And the men who will be the pallbearers, carrying the box to this spot, are listed by name: my two sons-in-law, two grandsons, and two nephews with whom I worked for a couple decades. They have already agreed to doing this.

You may think planning my funeral before I die would fall into a category of "overprogramming." I'd say it's more like a gift I'm giving the folks I will leave behind.

They will spend no time wondering, *What would Robert want?* There it will be—in black-and-white.

Without sounding like your grade-school teacher, your mother, or a drill sergeant, may I strongly encourage you to do the same?

While I was working on the manuscript for this book, I texted my buddy, Dr. Ray Ortlund, to tell him about this chapter regarding planning your own funeral service. He bounced right back with an email containing an attachment called "Funeral Service." Not surprisingly, Ray had already mapped out his own service.

Because I know this man, I'm not surprised by the

thoughtfulness of his planning. The reading of Scripture and hymns he loved are right there. A gift to his survivors.

Now, let me quickly say that creating this document is not meant to fence in my family. If they would like to call some audibles, they're welcome to. Even without my knowledge or permission. But doing this in advance does answer that question families must struggle with during a time of deep grief and loss: "What would my loved one want?" This is a kindness and a generous gift to those you leave behind.

LAUGHING AT DEATH

In addition to meaningful and inspiring Bible verses and hymns, the folks who attend your funeral are going to need to smile in the service. I've spoken at a few, and it's easy to get people to respond to happy stories with laughter, which always provides welcome relief.[6]

In 1999, I received a frantic phone call from a close friend who was a professional athlete. His agent's private jet had been reported to be in serious trouble. The suspicion was that the plane had lost pressure, the passengers and crew were dead, and the aircraft was flying on autopilot, headed for who knows where.

Also on the plane was Payne Stewart, the reigning U.S.

---

6. At Bobbie's funeral in November 2014, my daughters gave a tribute to their mother. They left some very sweet memories for us to enjoy. And they made us laugh. In fact, I had never seen a standing ovation for a eulogy. Until then. You can see for yourself (www.youtube.com/watch?v=Ze9nBp7jmWs). Or you can go to YouTube and search for "Bobbie Wolgemuth's Daughters' Testimony."

Open Champion, having just captured the crown at the storied Pinehurst Country Club in North Carolina.

Now, just a few months after his win at Pinehurst, Payne was on a private jet, flying out of Orlando, as it turned out, on autopilot. Because of a lack of oxygen, the six souls on the craft were dead. In a few hours, as the Lear 25 emptied its fuel tanks just across the North Dakota state line, the jet went screaming down, missiling into the ground at hundreds of miles an hour.

Airwaves around the world were filled with the story of this popular athlete's awful, spectacular demise. In a few days, through a flight and a series of introductions, I was in Orlando, sitting down with Paul Azinger, one of Payne's closest friends, who had been asked to deliver the eulogy. He had also been told that his remarks would be simulcast around the world, with a Super Bowl–size audience watching and listening. Paul asked me to draft the eulogy for him. I agreed.

The day before the service at the First Baptist Church, Paul and I visited the Stewart home. The purpose was to "borrow" a pair of Payne's argyle socks and one of his trademark tam o' shanter caps.

The script for Paul's remarks began with instructions I crafted for the speaker:

> Set script on the podium. Pull the cap out of your coat pocket, shake it into shape, and put it on. Step back and pull your pant legs up above your knees, revealing the argyles.

Now it was 10:00 a.m., Friday, October 29, 1999. The service had started. Michael W. Smith was singing. The folks scheduled to speak in the program were about to walk into the sanctuary. Paul turned to me, almost frantic. Taking me by the shoulders, he exclaimed, "I can't do it," he said just above a desperate whisper. "I can't do it."

With all the confidence I could muster, I replied, "Trust me, Paul. People will love it. People need to laugh at funerals."

Thankfully, Paul followed through on the plan. And as I had promised, sure enough, they loved it. First, they snickered as Paul did what we had agreed. He lifted his pant legs, exposing the argyles. They laughed. He pulled the hat out of his sport coat pocket, snapped it into shape, and put it on. The congregation broke out in vigorous applause.

Then Paul told the story of Payne firing up his brand-new bass boat in his garage, revving the outboard over and over, then without warning the whole thing bursting into flames.[7] Thankfully he had the presence of mind, and the strength, to lift the tongue of the trailer and push it into the driveway, thereby saving his house from sure destruction.

The people loved the story. They laughed. Again. Now they were ready to hear a message that included the gospel, plain and simple.

Paul turned the page of the script and began to read: "To try to accept the magnitude of this tragedy is the most difficult thing I've ever had to do. The void and the sadness we feel is real. But we are not alone in our mourning. The God of the universe joins us today in our sorrow."

For the next few minutes, Paul delivered his talk,

---

7. As you probably know, if your boat isn't in the water, starting the engine is a bad idea. Without hydration, the motor has no coolant, thus the flames. You may as well set down your fishing pole and pull out a stick and marshmallows.

honoring his friend and inspiring the thousands gathered and the millions watching on ESPN.

Paul closed his message with these words: "Whoever you are, wherever you are, whatever you've done, if you feel the tug of God's Spirit in your heart, do not turn away. If like Payne, Robert [Fraley] and Van [Arden] you want to know the happiness and peace that only Jesus Christ can bring, I invite you to confess your sin and receive Him as your Savior. Regardless of what your life has brought you, His love is enough. His peace is for real."[8]

When Paul was finished, the pastor of the church reminded the congregation that Payne was unashamed of his love for Jesus, then invited the ushers to come down the aisles and pass out "WWJD" rubber bracelets.[9] Something Payne wore night and day to announce his love for the Lord.

In fact, a few years later, I was in the merch tent at the Bay Hill Invitational golf tournament[10] in Orlando, purchasing a couple of golf shirts. The young man who was striking the keys on the cash register had something on his wrist. It was a WWJD rubber bracelet. I commented on it. He looked at me with a colossal grin. "I got this at Payne Stewart's funeral. I prayed to receive Jesus as my Savior in that service."

I walked around to the other side of the counter and hugged him. "So good to have you in the family," I said.

---

8. You can watch Paul Azinger's tribute to Payne Stewart on YouTube. Search for "Paul Azinger eulogy to Payne Stewart" (www.youtube.com/watch ?v=NiU_qb1gNvY).

9. What Would Jesus Do?

10. Now the Arnold Palmer Invitational (API).

MAKING THE FOLKS LAUGH
THROUGH THE TEARS

While I was drafting the manuscript for this book, veteran soldier and politician Senator Bob Dole passed away. The man was known for his dry, clever humor. At his service, a letter was read that Dole had composed for this moment. The congregation sat stoically at the awe-inspiring National Cathedral as the speaker—his daughter Robin—read Kansas's legendary leader's words:

> As I make the final walk on my life's journey, I do so without fear. Because I know that I will, again, not be walking alone. I know that God will be walking with me. I also confess that I'm a bit curious to learn and find if I am correct in thinking that Heaven will look a lot like Kansas and to see, like others who have gone before me, if I will still be able to vote in Chicago.

> The laughter was clearly audible. And don't you know that those friends enjoyed the relief of remembering the departed's wit.

LAUGHTER AT MY EXPENSE

If my daughters, Missy and Julie, are able to speak at my funeral—and I really hope they can—they will doubtless comb through their memory banks to come up with stuff that'll make the congregation laugh. Stuff at their daddy's expense.

Like the times when their mom would fix picnic dinner for the family, but instead of looking for a park, she'd bring the fixings to the office where I worked. Once a month after the company's financial statements were distributed, I'd literally spend the night there, preparing a summary report for my boss. Knowing this, my late wife, Bobbie, packed dinner in a basket, complete with a red-and-white-checkered tablecloth. The floor in my office became the grassy knoll, just perfect for a delicious meal.

Once we were finished, Missy and Julie would ask if we could play hide-and-seek. Because we did this every month, my answer was a sure thing. The girls would strike out into a maze of dark, narrow hallways that was this office. And then I'd go on a search-and-rescue mission. It makes me smile even now as I write these words decades later, to remember looking for them. Of course, I'd call their names as I searched. And when I'd get close, they would jump out and scare the daylights out of me. And when I'd holler it would scare them back. Good thing we were all by ourselves. Each time, our screams would collapse in hugs and laughter.

In addition to serious comments, I'm hoping the others who speak at my funeral can come up with their own stories of "Robert's antics" to share and remember together. To laugh with love and delight.

SOMETHING ELSE FOR THE SERVICE

In December 2021, Nancy and I attended a memorial service in Southern California for our dear friend Al Sanders.

One of the pioneers of Christian Radio, Al is remembered by colleagues in this way: "Al was ever creative, humorous, generous, attentive, compassionate, and always unswerving in his spiritual commitment." The service included singing a few of Al's favorite hymns, elegantly accompanied on the piano by his beloved Margaret—Al's wife of seventy-three years.[11]

Thankfully, the lyrics to each verse were projected onto a screen in front of us so we could keep up. One of the hymns, "There Is a Fountain Filled with Blood," written by William Cowper in 1772, brought tears to many eyes. Especially the fifth verse:

When this poor, lisping, stamm'ring tongue
Lies silent in the grave,
Then in a nobler, sweeter song
I'll sing Thy pow'r to save:
I'll sing Thy pow'r to save,
I'll sing Thy pow'r to save;
Then in a nobler, sweeter song,
I'll sing Thy pow'r to save.[12]

One of the reasons this verse evoked emotions from so many of us was that Al Sanders possessed a voice that was anything but poor, lisping, or stammering. He was, in fact, the welcoming "voice" of many popular radio broadcasts, especially pastor Chuck Swindoll's "Insight for Living."

Halfway through the service, the host invited Al's

---

11. This is not a misprint.
12. William Cowper, "There Is a Fountain Filled with Blood" (1772). Public domain.

grandchildren to the platform. One at a time, they stepped to the podium, and each of them read one of Al's favorite Bible passages. Since I was in the process of drafting the manuscript for this book and was eager to help you with ideas for your funeral, I made a note on my phone to include this list.

One by one, they read the following passages:

- ◆ Psalm 23
- ◆ 2 Corinthians 4:16–18
- ◆ 2 Corinthians 5:17–20
- ◆ 1 Thessalonians 4:13–18
- ◆ Revelation 22:4–5—the glorious snapshot of Heaven

Hearing these young voices and watching their poise as they carefully read God's Holy Word out loud in honor of their grandfather was magnificent. Such a nice idea!

WHAT REALLY MATTERS
AT YOUR SERVICE

Before tying a bow—or in this case, closing the lid—on this chapter, there are a few important things I'd encourage you to remember about planning your funeral service.

People who leave their homes and travel across the world to minister hope and salvation in Christ will always be heroes to me. Having spent a few years on the mission field as a kid and having parents who often hosted missionaries in our home, I remember hearing the name C. T. Studd[13] as a kid. Clarence Thomas (C. T.) had been a decorated athlete in his country when he attended a rally where the revivalist D. L. Moody was preaching. C. T. was radically converted and eventually traveled to China and then to Africa, boldly telling of his love for the Lord. Stepping into Heaven in 1931, C. T. surely heard his Lord welcome him with, "Well done, good and faithful servant!"

One of Studd's most famous quotes ought to be our goal for the thing that people will remember most about our life as they drive home after our funeral service: "Only one life, 'twill soon be past, only what's done for Christ will last."[14]

How good is this?

Of course, catching up on what they didn't know about us will be important in our funerals, as will remembering with joy who we were, but their hearts will need to be alerted to what was really important to us, especially our love for our family, friends, and Jesus Christ, maybe even with an opportunity to welcome Him into their lives, just as we have done.

My greatest desire is that people who drive back to their homes after my service will remember me as a broken and sinful man who, by God's grace, was ushered into His presence.

King David, who really did have a way with words, penned it like this:

---

13. What young man wouldn't like to have the name "Studd"?
14. C. T. Studd, "Only One Life," Poetry about Jesus and Salvation, http://cavaliersonly.com/poetry_by_christian_poets_of_the_past/only_one_life_twill_soon_be_past_-_poem_by_ct_studd.

FINISH LINE

You make known to me the path of life;
 you will fill me with joy in your presence,
 with eternal pleasures at your right hand.
  (Psalm 16:11)

NINE

NO MORE SECRETS

So David made extensive preparations before his death.

"I bought a casket today."

FROM MY PERSONAL JOURNAL,
SEPTEMBER 2014

G iven my lifetime line of work, I've had the privilege of meeting a number of well-known people. Frankly, I confess that it's always been a challenge to not mention the names of these individuals in casual conversations, clearly with the intent of impressing whomever I was speaking to. Sometimes they seemed impressed. More often they changed the subject to something about which they actually cared.

World-renowned thinker, apologist, speaker, and author Ravi Zacharias was my friend. By that, I don't mean we met once in a green room. He really was my friend.

As a teen living in India, Ravi was converted to Christ under my father Samuel Wolgemuth's ministry. They were very close. Ravi and I often remarked that we shared a father—mine by flesh and blood, his spiritually. My own siblings and their mates also had this visceral connection with Ravi and his wife, Margie.

As his literary agent, I was involved in nearly every book he wrote. Negotiating, along with my colleagues, the publishers' contracts. Ravi and I texted often, even when he was globetrotting. Especially when he was globetrotting.

The week he died, in the spring of 2020, I studied photos his family posted on social media, especially the ones at the close of his life. I wept at the sight of my failing friend.

I spoke at length by phone with Margie. She was, of course, crushed by the passing of her beloved. I prayed with her.

But in the months that followed, troubling things about Ravi began to surface. Like what happens when you notice one of the front wheels of your car pulling right or left, showing signs of misalignment. Troubling news began to seep from his ministry associates. Bad news about a life it seemed Ravi was living in the dark. It was clear that neither anyone in his family nor ministry colleagues had any idea of this shadowed stuff.

As the awful accounts of his hidden life surfaced, many hearts broke. Not just for the millions who had been impacted by his brilliance and his winsomeness, but for me.

Although not by any stretch as much as his family suffered, I hurt. I even felt a thin slice of betrayal.

I mention Ravi for one reason only. It's the point of this chapter. A point I hope you and I never forget.

When we die, people are going to go through our things. Lots of people. All our things. Every single shred. Of everything.

Stuff we squirreled away in desks and closets or in cardboard boxes in the attic or basement or in storage. These are going to be foraged. This includes receipts we've saved and other little scraps of paper hiding in shoeboxes. This treasure hunt also includes electronic documents and things we've done online. People we've spoken to . . . or emailed . . . or texted will come forward, disclosing words we spoke or wrote to them.

Jesus referred to this unvarnished reality: "There is nothing concealed that will not be disclosed, or hidden that will not be made known. What you have said in the dark will be heard in the daylight, and what you have whispered in the ear in the inner rooms will be proclaimed from the roofs" (Luke 12:2–3).

The first sentence of a little song we sang in Sunday school reminded us. We pretended our index finger was a candle, and our other hand a bushel cupped over the candle. "Hide it under a bushel? No! I'm going to let it shine."

Again Jesus said, "No one lights a lamp and hides it in a clay jar or puts it under a bed. Instead, they put it on a stand, so that those who come in can see the light. For there is nothing hidden that will not be disclosed, and nothing concealed that will not be known or brought out into the open" (Luke 8:16–17).

In the context of the hiding of our stuff while we're alive and the truth that people *will* comb through everything after we're dead, these verses together are like a fastball screaming toward our chins. A wake-up call on steroids. Because He is God, Jesus knows about folks pilfering through our goodies after our bodies are no longer 98.6 degrees. When we're dead, there will be no more secrets.

The message here could be several-fold. First, I could encourage you to do a really good job of destroying "documents and things" or putting them in a place where no one will find them. Maybe digging a hole in a remote forest and burying them. Neither of these are what I have in mind. Second, and this really is the message, *turn the light on while you're alive*. Search these things. How much better for you to be holding the flashlight as the living peel back through your life.

> TURN THE LIGHT ON WHILE YOU'RE ALIVE. SEARCH THESE THINGS. HOW MUCH BETTER TO BE HOLDING THE FLASHLIGHT AS THE LIVING PEEL BACK THROUGH YOUR LIFE.

There are menacing things that surely will be tangled without your explanation. Don't wait until you can't explain them. And there may be—will be—things to confess.

In 2005, two of my nephews joined the literary agency I had founded fifteen years earlier with my dear friend, Michael Hyatt. Five years before I hired these young men, Mike and I agreed that he was going to step back into the corporate world and I would buy and carry the company on my own. This I did for seven years, until the workload was too much to carry by myself. As it turned out, my brother

Dan's sons, Andrew and Erik, were the happy answer, and I invited them to join me.

This turned out to be one of the brilliant decisions of my business life. I'm humbled by the amazing way it has turned out—all by God's grace.

On their first day, these twentysomething men stood in front of me. I was sitting at my desk and they were listening to me waxing wise about the business of which they were now a part. I scooted my chair back a little so I could look down to see the drawers to my right and left. Pointing to them, I told these bright young men that they were welcome to open these drawers anytime they were looking for something. Turning to the credenza behind me, I pointed to the drawers and said the same thing. My computer was also there, and I assured them that there was nothing secret inside. I nodded toward the closet across the room and repeated, "Nothing in there you can't dig through."

I draw you into this moment, not to brag about how transparent I am, but to confess that I'd rather have an under-the-radar life. It would be a lot more fun to be able to enjoy salacious and satisfying stuff to feed my mind, to tantalize my affections in secret. And because this is true, because it would be so easy to fall, I have intentionally dragged big, heavy barricades around my mind and heart to keep me squared away. Knowing that anyone at any time has my blessing to dig through anything provides a sort of hedge around leaving stinky garbage in these places.

"Don't you have the raw discipline to do this without these barricades, Robert?" you might ask.

No, I don't.

From the moment of my conception, I've had a "heart murmur." A sinful flaw built in, and I know it. In fact, the Old Testament prophet Jeremiah must have had the same: "The heart is more deceitful than anything else, and incurable—who can understand it?" (17:9 CSB).

For many years, one of the blockades I've wrestled into place to surround my heart is giving everyone in my life full-access, backstage passes to it all. When I'm dead, they're going to be able to rummage through everything. I have already issued permission and would hate for this to be a bad experience for them. Having people I love find surprising things. Even though my skin will be cold and gray and my calcifying mind won't be aware of their discoveries, I'd rather save myself—and my family—the postmortem embarrassment by keeping my secret files clear of any trash right now.

Even as I write these words, I'm taking inventory. Is what I'm saying absolutely true? Are there any skeletons? Any hidden things or unresolved treacheries in there? Do I have any relationships waiting for a confession from me? Is there anyone? Anyone I'm resenting? Or avoiding. Or hating?

Oh, how I wish I could draw you into my quiet study right now. Except for a little classical music playing in the background, it's silent in here. Just a few feet away is a comfortable couch. It's actually one of those split pieces that gives two occupants the freedom to separately recline. Nancy and I sit here to watch the news or a movie. But it's free now. For you.

Now I'm inviting you in. Let's take the scrapbook of our lives, drop them onto our laps, and turn the big, heavy, photo-thick pages together. We can laugh at silly things like the turquoise leisure suit I was wearing in the 1970s or the long hair hanging below my ears. Your pictures include some laughable ones too.

Then we talk about our lives. Decisions we made. Words we spoke. Relationships that started well but descended into rancor and separation. Lumps form in our throats, realizing some of the foolishness. There's regret. And pain.

"This is hard," I say, "but when we're dead and gone, someone else is going to go through this scrapbook, so let's page through it while we're alive. Together. Might as well look now."

You agree.

Suddenly and without any warning, Jesus shows up. In our minds, He is standing here. Right in my study. So now it's three of us. You, me, and the Lord. He's completely familiar with everything we've been talking about. Pages from the scrapbook that have made us laugh. And cry. And rejoice. And regret. What does He say?

A long time ago, Jesus' disciples were holding a secret meeting, kind of like the one you and I are having in my study. The Eleven[1] were physically exhausted by the cascade of events brought on in recent days. There had been the Passover meal in the upper room, Judas's betrayal, Peter's denial, the mock trial, the crowd calling for Jesus' crucifixion, Pilate's cowardice, the awful parade to Calvary, the gruesome execution, the days of despair because Jesus was gone, the empty tomb, and the testimony of the women who saw it.

---

1. Judas's lifeless corpse was hanging at the business end of a rope.

It was like the disciples were paging through the memories, just as you and I have been.

Here's how Luke describes it, just as his friends had told him: "While they were still talking about this, Jesus himself stood among them and said to them, 'Peace be with you.' They were startled and frightened, thinking they saw a ghost" (Luke 24:36–37).

Startled? Of course. Embarrassed because they had ditched their Friend, running for their lives? Probably.

Let's go back to my study and experience for ourselves the wonder of Jesus showing up. Like the disciples, we are surprised. Alarmed. And knowing what we've just been doing, paging back through the memories of our lives, what does He say to us? Knowing and understanding it all?

He says to us what He said to His friends in that upper room: "Peace be with you."

Then just like it is with you and me and our scrapbooks, these men and the very Son of God review the past events together. Jesus speaks: "This is what I told you while I was still with you: Everything must be fulfilled that is written about me in the Law of Moses, the Prophets and the Psalms" (Luke 24:44).

These men must have been more than a little chagrined about what they were recalling, just as you and I may feel as we page through the history of our lives—the successes and the failures. But Jesus broke through the tangle of their regrets and embarrassments with four words you and I need to hear: *"Peace be with you."*

Then, like my Apple watch tickling my wrist with "Time to Stand" every hour or so, admonishing me to get off my duff and get some fresh air, Jesus suggests we go for a walk.

As we're outside, breathing in gulps of clean oxygen, we chat about the regrets we've just reviewed. Some of the things that will be discovered when we're dead. There's stuff in there that includes wrongs committed against us. And Jesus' words come back to our conscious minds: "If your brother sins against you, go tell him his fault, between you and him alone. If he listens to you, you have won your brother" (Matthew 18:15 CSB).

And we are gripped by the times we screwed up. These memories pour in. Again, Jesus' favorite disciple, who's walking along with us, reminds us of what Jesus said about this: "If we confess our sins, he is faithful and just and will forgive us our sins and purify us from all unrighteousness" (1 John 1:9).

Or how about David's response after thumbing through his own scrapbook:

> LORD, if you kept a record of our sins,
>   who, O Lord, could ever survive?
> But you offer forgiveness,
>   that we might learn to fear you. (Psalm 130:3–4 NLT)

What has the experience of paging through our lives' memories revealed? Troubling things done to us? Foolish things we've done to others?

Before our survivors have a chance to discover the tedious details of our histories after we're gone, we can do the review ourselves. Now, while we can. And then we will be able, as they used to say, to clear the air.

You may be a bullet-point person. If so, right here in my study I've boiled down five steps to experiencing the peace Jesus spoke to us:

- **REVEAL.** Carefully review your past. Honestly assess every relationship you've had. Especially the hard ones. Every event you can remember. Go through your closets, desks, attic, cardboard boxes, computer files.
- **ADMIT.** Lift these things up so they can "get air." Like a diver holding up a treasure he's just found under the water.
- **CONFESS.** James must have unearthed something in his life. Why else would he have jotted down these words: "Confess your sins to each other and pray for each other so that you may be healed" (5:16)?
- **FORGIVE.** Whether it's about others or yourself, say these words out loud: "I forgive you." Or "Would you please forgive me?"
- **RELEASE.** "As far as the east is from the west, so far has he removed our transgressions from us" (Psalm 103:12).

The message is clear. You and I have stuff in our personal history. Some embarrassing things on our mental hard drive that we'd like to hide. So before our heirs go rummaging through our things after we're gone, let's start with a video of God going through them with us first.

We know that nothing we find together will be a surprise

to Him. No one will ever hear Him say, "Hey, what's that doing in here? I didn't know about *that*."

When Adam and Eve disobeyed God in the Garden of Eden and they heard the sound of His footsteps, they hid. And God asked a rhetorical question: "Where are you?" (Genesis 3:9). Rhetorical because He knew exactly where they were. Just like He knows what's in those cardboard boxes, in the back of your closets, and on your hard drives.

Remember what the coach used to say when the boys stood around one of their teammates who had just been clocked in the head or had the wind knocked out of him. "Stand back, men. Give him air." As though the oxygen was being depleted by the presence of the boys surrounding their comrade. In any case, this is what I'd encourage you to do—actually, I'd plead with you to do: Give this stuff air.

> SO BEFORE OUR HEIRS GO RUMMAGING THROUGH OUR THINGS AFTER WE'RE GONE, LET'S START WITH A VIDEO OF GOD GOING THROUGH THEM WITH US FIRST.

Those things you have not disclosed or confessed or made right must have air to breathe. Space enough for you to address, explain, or say you're sorry for.

While I was writing this chapter, Nancy told me about a longtime friend who had gone through his parents' effects after they died at ninety-two and ninety years of age. Here's how he described the experience to Nancy: "I spent an entire month sorting through a lifetime of their accumulated stuff—correspondence, financial data, clippings, photos, and on and on. It was an almost complete record of their lives."

When it was all said and done, after poring through the massive collection of memorabilia and paperwork, this son observed with a sense of wonder, "There was not one single thing in my parents' belongings that was inconsistent with the profession of their relationship with Christ."

How would you fare if someone were to go through the record of your life—all your possessions, the books and magazines you've read, the movies you've rented, your financial records, tax returns, journals, calendar, phone bills, correspondence, texts and emails, a record of all your cell phone and internet activity? The sobering thing is that once you and I are dead, they will.

When my children or grandchildren clear out my garage or my study or the boxes in our storage unit, I desperately want them to say the same thing Nancy's friend said about what his parents left behind.

After Bobbie died in 2014, I was forced to do some of this evaluating over the course of the next year. In fact, because I wasn't just moving everything from one house to another but rather was exploding disbursing my goods from my house to five different locations, I had no choice but to unpack and repack everything. One trailer was going to my little house in Charlotte; one to my daughter Julie's house also in Charlotte; one to my daughter Missy's house in Greenville; one to Nancy's house in Michigan, which I moved to in late 2015; and one to my colleagues' offices in Denver.

After doing all of this reviewing, my slate was clean. The swamp had been drained so the gators were visible. I was able to deal with each one. Everything in my files, my cardboard boxes, and closets was examined and tossed . . . or purposely kept. Ironically—and not surprisingly—by now I've accumulated some more boxes, a full closet, and a couple storage units to dig through. Which I promise to do again by the time this book is published.

THEY DON'T WANT YOUR STUFF

As of the time of this writing, my older sister, Ruth, is eighty-one. It's a long story, but my relationship with this sister is special. When we were kids living with our parents on the mission field,[2] my three siblings and I traveled 75 miles each way to an American Christian school—a one-mile walk, a ten-minute bus ride, two trains with an intermediate stop in a very busy station, topped off with a two-mile walk. I was in first grade, Ken in third, Sam in fifth, and Ruth in seventh. Guess who was in charge of this little troupe? That's right, Ruth. A seventh grader, 150 miles each day, shepherding her three young brothers. Safely. Is it any wonder I love this woman so much?

In any case, Ruth and I recently talked about downsizing our stuff in preparation for our last breath. Like many women her age, Ruth has some expensive collections, including two glass-doored cabinets full of priceless (at least to her) cut-glass figurines.

When she and her three grown children talked about these treasures, and everything else in Ruth and Stan's home, one of their sons said simply this: "You've seen those huge

---

2. We were in Japan for a two-year assignment with Youth for Christ.

dumpsters, Mom? The ones they winch up on the back of an 18-wheeler? Well, when you're gone, we're putting one of those in your driveway."[3]

I have seen the way Ruth treats her crystal. It takes her forever to dust them, one delicate creature at a time. Imagine these treasures being tossed into a trash dumpster. The same is likely true for you. It may feel heartbreaking, but it is very likely your kids and grandkids don't want your stuff.

Nancy and I have had this conversation with many folks our age. One friend in particular has an amazing collection of Hummel figurines. "Hundreds of them," she says. And she whines that her children and grandchildren have no interest. None. Her kids and grandkids don't want her stuff.

A question for you and me: Have we embraced the fact that when we die, most of what we have will be forgotten? Completely ignored? We have no choice in this. It will happen. No one wants our stuff.

MERGE AND PURGE

Having had the up-close-and-personal joy of being introduced and then connected to Nancy's Revive Our Hearts (ROH) ministry, I was reminded of the necessary process that all nonprofits experience—that of systematically going through their computer records of donors. When you hear about ministries that do this, you become aware of the expression "active and inactive donors." And the need to

---

3. This may sound like Ruth's children are angry or cruel. Unkind to their mother. Not true. They're fantastic. They just don't want her stuff. Not at all.

electronically comb through—and then purge—records for people who may have had an interest at one time but have not been heard from for years.

More often than not, these folks have been connected to ROH by surface mail or electronic correspondence. Some want to stay in contact, and some don't. Some people once enjoyed regular communiques, but now, for whatever reason, they no longer welcome the correspondence. Nancy's team always gives them a chance to opt out, and it's important that these people's wishes are honored.

Nearly every electronic solicitation I receive gives me a chance to "unsubscribe." In fact, giving people the opportunity to do this is a Federal Trade Commission law called the "Can-Spam Act."[4] This directive sets the rules for commercial email, establishes requirements for commercial messages, gives recipients the right to request that you stop emailing them, and spells out tough penalties for violations.

Before you and I die, when it will be too late to merge/purge our histories, here's a chance to achieve what's known as "list hygiene"—cleaning out the deadbeat stuff back there in our files.[5] The time we take now to get this done will provide our loved ones more peace than we can imagine.

This is all part of the process of our journey. It's the discipline of embracing the fact that there's a lot more sand

---

4. "Can-Spam Act: A Compliance Guide for Business," Federal Trade Commission, accessed June 30, 2022, www.ftc.gov/tips-advice/business-center/guidance/can-spam-act-compliance-guide-business.

5. Because of the nature of electronic media, some files are not erasable. If you're not an expert at determining this, I encourage you to find someone who knows more about it than you do. Identifying a person who is more adept at technology than you are will not be difficult. Right?

below the narrow in our hourglass than above it. Moses, Israel's earthly redeemer, encouraged us in the book of Psalms to get serious about this reality when he wrote, "Teach us to number our days, that we may gain a heart of wisdom" (90:12).

TEN

DYING

We want more than pain control and a clean bed. We hope to die well.

KATY BUTLER, *THE ART OF DYING WELL*

It is good to look death in the eye and constantly remind ourselves that our hope is in God, who defeated death.

ROB MOLL, *THE ART OF DYING*

In the same way you and I talked about planning our funerals, this would be a good time to talk about the thing that'll make our funerals necessary. Dying.

For almost the entire fourth year of our marriage, Nancy and I focused on this preparation. With the crisp thinking of our attorney to shepherd us, we talked about our own end-of-life issues. These conversations were not easy to navigate.

Sobriety was in order, that's for sure. I mean, there's no space for levity when a professional asks you the question about whether or not you want your doctors to use heroic means to try to keep you alive, whether you want "DNR"[1] stamped on your documents.

A LITTLE HELP FROM MY FRIENDS

In preparing to write this book, I logged into Amazon and purchased a bunch of books. They were all helpful. Some more than others.

Except for the one written by Rob Moll,[2] which I really loved, the most insightful were the ones written by medical doctors and pastors whose lives were immersed in the experiences of treating those who were dying. Some wrote of the challenges of dealing with families that had differing opinions about the treatment of a loved one on the threshold of eternity. Sometimes these conflicts were out in the open. Others were more hidden, but plenty insidious.

Before going any further into this subject, I'd like to start with the assumption that these differences had nothing at all to do with the survivor's love for the dying person. Theirs was a conundrum that did not relate to loving or not loving the one who was near death. In every case I read, the challenge was always this: *What is the most loving thing to do here?* For the dying. And for us.

---

1. Do Not Resuscitate.
2. Rob Moll, *The Art of Dying: Living Fully into the Life to Come* (Downers Grove, IL: InterVarsity, 2010).

But even more consequential than this question is the one I hope to answer in this chapter. It's taking the time to determine what we want our survivors to know about what we want them to do when we're dying. Or not to do.

When this question is unanswered and the expiring person has lost the ability to clearly articulate their wishes, that's when conflict is born. Because you and I are walking through this together, my hope is that the fog will lift and the sun will shine on the answer to this question: "What does [place your name here] want us to do now?"

> IT'S TAKING THE TIME TO DETERMINE WHAT WE WANT OUR SURVIVORS TO KNOW ABOUT WHAT WE WANT THEM TO DO WHEN WE'RE DYING. OR NOT TO DO.

In February 2012, when Bobbie was diagnosed with stage IV ovarian cancer, even before she was fully awake after the surgery that revealed the vicious disease lurking inside her, my daughters and I resolved the following declarations, which we repeated many times when people we loved asked how we were handling the news.

- We are not angry.
- We are not afraid.
- Although we were surprised by the news, we know our loving Father was not.
- Because of the above, we are treating this as a gift, which by definition is always unknown by the recipient.
- Our only goal is that God will be praised through the process and the outcome, and that because suffering is

the money of the gospel, many will be exposed to the Good News because of our journey.

These five things guided us over the next thirty months of treatments, short-lived victories, and ultimately Bobbie's death. Looking back, we could not be more grateful for these anchors. Like stepping-stones across a rushing river, they became safe places for our thinking.

Once Bobbie was awake, we talked through some knotty issues. Especially, where do we go from here?

THE LAST STAGE OUT OF TOWN

In 1969, a seminal work titled *On Death and Dying* was published.[3] The book's author was Elisabeth Kübler-Ross, a Swiss-American psychiatrist. In this volume she identified the five stages of death—an explanation that has become the standard for people in the same place where my family and I found ourselves.

The diagnosis has been announced. The patient is terminal. The chance that this diagnosis is flawed is slim. How is the one who is sick supposed to respond? And what are we to do?

Here's how I would summarize Kübler-Ross's stages when a death sentence is pronounced:[4]

---

3. Elisabeth Kübler-Ross, *On Death and Dying: What the Dying Have to Teach Doctors, Nurses, Clergy, and Their Own Families*, 50th anniv. ed. (New York: Scribner, 2019).

4. I'm paraphrasing here from a resource located on the Huntington's Disease Society of America website, https://hdsa.org/wp-content/uploads/2015/02/13080.pdf.

DYING

1. **DENIAL:** "I feel fine. This cannot be happening—not to me." Denial is usually only a temporary defense for the individual. A sequence of affirming diagnoses seals the facts, thus denial fades. Like a sniper's bullet, the surprise shot that was fired becomes real.

2. **ANGER:** "Why me? It's not fair. Who's to blame for this?" In this second stage, the person realizes that denial cannot continue. Because of anger, the dying person can be very difficult to care for because of misplaced feelings of rage and envy.

3. **BARGAINING:** "Just let me live to see my children graduate. Or get married. Or have children of their own." Usually, the negotiation for an extended life is made with a higher power in exchange for a reformed lifestyle. Psychologically, the person is saying, "I understand I will die, but if I could just have more time . . ."

4. **DEPRESSION:** "I'm so sad, why bother with anything? I'm going to die; what's the point?" In this stage, the person may become silent, refuse visitors, and spend much of the time grieving and crying. As protection, this process allows the dying one to disconnect from anything that smacks of love and affection.

5. **ACCEPTANCE:** "It's going to be okay. I can't fight it; I might as well prepare for it." In this last stage, the person begins to come to terms with their mortality.

These stages were drafted by a person who made no claim to see life—or death—through the prism of a biblical worldview. For Kübler-Ross, a deity that can be known doesn't exist or actually count in the equation.

But for the sake of this conversation with you, I've tackled the idea of what these stages would look like coming from a person who loves Jesus and has committed his life—and death—to the veracity of God's Word and the realities of life—and death—with Him.

That would be me.

Assuming these stages are real, what if you and I cling to Scripture's revelation—a Creator, God's Word as truth, the reality of sin and separation from God, repentance and salvation as real—rather than as a temporary bromide viewed with cynical suspicion. What is God's answer when we face these stages ourselves?

As you know, I'm not a medical doctor, a clinically seasoned counselor, a seminary-trained pastor, or a scholar. As I often say, I'm just an ordinary guy trying to stay in his lane, walking down the sidewalk with you. I'm only speaking with you, my friend, at a corner table over a cup of coffee. In the absence of professional training on any of the above specialties, I can assure you that there are plenty of experts whose work is thoroughly accessible. And, of course, I celebrate your exploration of these.

But as a layman who has soaked in the realities of life and death, I'm going to venture out, with your permission, and look at these five stages through my lens. The prism of a Christian man unwrapping his own journey, fully embracing his mortality and the mortality of those he loves, and searching for meaning and answers taken from his own experience and from the Bible.

DENIAL

I feel fine. This cannot be happening—not to me.

Though we desperately try to look the other way when
we receive terminal news, there's clearly no turning back.
When Tim Keller was diagnosed with pancreatic cancer in
the winter of 2020, he wrote, "Despite my rational, conscious
acknowledgment that I would die someday, the shattering
reality of a fatal diagnosis provoked a remarkably strong
psychological denial of mortality."[5]

Wherever you are, as you read Tim's words, they ring
true, don't they?

Deeply grateful for the way she responds to all kinds of
news—good or tragic—my wife Nancy's life verse is Luke
1:38, the account of the angel's visitation to the young virgin
Mary and Mary's response to the outrageous pronouncement
that she is to conceive a Baby, not the result of human pas-
sion, but by way of the Holy Spirit.

Nancy sums this verse up in two simple words: *Yes,
Lord!* If there were a trademark that's seared into her life
and ministry, it would surely be this: "Yes, Lord!"

If Kübler-Ross begins her list of stages of grief with, "No
way," then our response can be, "Yes, Lord!"

In my own experience, even though denial is a human
response, a natural pushback from awful news about me or
someone I love, faith's confident response can be a lifeline.

Here's something from the Bible that talks back so clearly
to the temptation to denial:

5. Timothy Keller, "Growing My Faith in the Face of Death," *Atlantic*,
March 7, 2021, www.theatlantic.com/ideas/archive/2021/03/tim-keller-growing
-my-faith-face-death/618219.

Who shall separate us from the love of Christ? Shall trouble or hardship or persecution or famine or nakedness or danger or sword? As it is written:

> "For your sake we face death all day long;
> we are considered as sheep to be
> slaughtered."

No, in all these things we are more than conquerors through him who loved us. (Romans 8:35–37)

Didn't the apostle Paul nail it here? Sometimes text lifted from the Bible needs some scholarly interpretation. Not this time.

To his list—trouble, hardship, persecution, famine, nakedness, danger, sword—Paul could have added cancer, heart attack, stroke, pandemic, virus, car accident.

As followers of Christ, we do not stick our heads in the sand or pull a heavy blanket over reality. Instead, we embrace God's providence. In the fall of 2019, Nancy and I wrote our first book together, *You Can Trust God to Write Your Story*.[6] What we wrote, we meant at the time. And then when 2020 came, our resolve was put to the test. What with a global pandemic and two cancers visited on my body, we repeated this declaration to each other maybe a thousand times. Was it true? Was God trustworthy? Really?

Yes.

Denial's greatest adversary is trust.

---

6. Robert and Nancy Wolgemuth, *You Can Trust God to Write Your Story: Embracing the Mysteries of Providence* (Chicago: Moody, 2019).

ANGER

Why me? It's not fair. Who's to blame for this?

Over the centuries a lot has been written about anger. Even the Bible includes quite a bit of ink related to this subject. So if I'm walking with Christ and facing a bleak diagnosis, can I get mad? Or if my wife's diagnosis includes "stage IV," is it okay to fire off? You know, somehow get even with this bad news?

Consider these words from the apostle Paul:

> Be angry and do not sin; do not let the sun go down on your anger, and give no opportunity to the devil. (Ephesians 4:26–27 ESV)

You may want to double-check this with your pastor, but I believe that anger can become "sin" when it's directed at one of God's creatures. But I do think it's permissible to get really ticked off at sin and the destruction it causes everywhere. And you can get mad at sickness. And terminal disease. And Satan, the horrible creature who is the author of sin.

After the snake tempted Eve and lied to Adam, God was demonstrably furious and let the snake have it:

> So the LORD God said to the serpent, "Because you have done this,
>
> 'Cursed are you above all livestock
> and all wild animals!
> You will crawl on your belly

and you will eat dust
all the days of your life.'" (Genesis 3:14)

I remember positioning myself behind the steering wheel of my car in the M. D. Anderson parking lot in the late afternoon of February 14, 2012, and shouting at the top of my lungs, "I hate cancer." That day I learned that my wife was in the crosshairs of a death sentence.

God understood.

BARGAINING
Just let me live to see my children graduate. Or get married. Or have children of their own.

Negotiating is a first cousin to denial. And it really hits home.

In the late summer of 2014, as Bobbie's cancer grew more severe, our granddaughter Abby, then a college student, asked if she could bring her boyfriend home to meet "Nanny." There is not enough room here to adequately describe Bobbie and Abby's relationship. Let me take a run at it anyway. Before Abby was two, Bobbie could tell she loved music. And singing.

Even at this young age, Abby not only could carry a tune, but she had a sweet, on-pitch voice. So armed with a kitchen spatula, Bobbie taught her granddaughter how to hold a microphone and sing and visually connect with an audience. From that came four musical recordings for *Hymns for a Kid's Heart*, with Bobbie and Joni Eareckson Tada. Abby did many of the vocals on that four-book and CD series. These were recorded before Abby turned eight. She was also the youngest singing guest in the studio at Focus on the Family with Dr. James Dobson. All this because Bobbie had noticed this little lady could sing.

So when Abby asked if she could bring her boyfriend to Orlando to meet Bobbie, we realized that, even though they had only been dating a few months, if, in fact, they did marry, this might be the only chance Ben would have to meet his possible Nanny-in-law. Abby's precious grandma Bobbie. Ben made the visit. It was a good idea.

As you'd understand, this love for Abby magnified Bobbie's eagerness to see her precious granddaughter marry and to be able to attend the wedding herself. As it turned out, this was an event she missed by nineteen months. Bobbie slipped into glory on October 28, 2014. In May 2016, Abby and Ben married. And then on January 13, 2022, their little boy, Ezra Dean Quirin, was born.

Bobbie missed Abby's wedding and the birth of her first great-grandchild, exactly what Elisabeth Kübler-Ross had suggested—"just let me live to see my children get married and have children." And I know that when the cancer diagnosis was deadly, Bobbie deeply mourned the prospective eventuality of this loss.

Even though Bobbie, this remarkable woman, wept over this reality, she fully embraced the sweetness and surety of God's providence. And she testified of this to every one of her visitors.

In early 2014, Bobbie agreed to participate in a clinical trial that might prove to be helpful for women she would never meet. I watched her suffer through indescribable effects of this medical experiment. She never stopped smiling.

With a twinkle in her eye, she would challenge the women in her Bible study group to choose "no complain" weeks. And I am a witness to the fact that she earned gold stars in this discipline herself.

DEPRESSION

I'm so sad, why bother with anything? I'm going to die; what's the point?

This emotion is real. Some Christians may believe that depression is sin. In fact, isolation and silent agony were modeled by no less than the sinless Jesus Christ Himself.

The Savior, God in human flesh, knew the pain and suffering and death that was waiting for Him. And I believe that His Father listened tenderly to Jesus' cries in Gethsemane and on the cross without suggesting that His only begotten Son "snap out of it."

Only God knew that Bobbie's attitude in facing her diagnosis and prognosis would provide a template for me just a few years later when I was faced with my own cancer journey. Like an apprentice standing close by a craftsman, parroting their every move, I learned from my wife's attitude. *I can do this*, I repeated to myself silently. *I've seen this before, and I can do it.* But this was not blathering, flaccid motivational self-talk; it was absolute confidence in a God Bobbie knew. And, again, a Sovereign she trusted.

Like a child crossing a busy street, Bobbie held Jesus' hand. She took her cues and her confidence from Him. Ask anyone who watched her handle this, and they'll surely corroborate my account.

ACCEPTANCE

It's going to be okay. I can't fight it; I might as well prepare for it.

In this last stage, we begin to come to terms with our mortality. Again, the model for this acceptance is Jesus. Suspended between Heaven and earth, the nails ripping the flesh of His hands and feet, the Savior embraced the reality of His death and the safety of His Father's care, as expressed in the words of the psalmist David:

> You are my refuge.
> Into your hands I commit my spirit;
> deliver me, LORD, my faithful God.
> (Psalm 31:4–5)

Don't you love the sweetness of the relationship between Jesus and His Father? Jesus knew His Father to be His "refuge." His very own hiding place. In fact, from the cross, Jesus quoted the words of King David ("Into your hands I commit my spirit"[7]), who, a thousand years before, had referred to the same Lord as his Good Shepherd.[8] Moments before a death He knew all about, Jesus embraced His mortality. And clung to His Father. His Shepherd.

How many stories have you heard about terminal folks forecasting and embracing the certainty as well as the timing of their deaths? My own account includes Bobbie telling our daughters late at night, October 27, 2014, just a few hours before her death, "I'm going to die tomorrow morning."

---

7. Luke 23:46.
8. See Psalm 23.

At 10:40 the next morning, she did.

You and I don't know how we will die. As a man, it may happen suddenly, soon after my friends hear me say, "Hey, you guys. Watch this." If you're a woman, it'll likely be something else. As I mentioned in chapter 7, 7 percent of us will die suddenly. The exit ramp for 93 percent will be protracted. It may be years, months, weeks, or just days.

WHEN YOU AND I KNOW WITH ABSOLUTE CERTAINTY THAT OUR END IS NEAR, GOD HIMSELF WILL BE OUR REFUGE. OUR STRENGTH. THE LORD ALMIGHTY WILL BE WITH US.

When you and I know with absolute certainty that our end is near, God Himself will be our refuge. Our strength. The Lord Almighty will be with us.[9]

Armed with this truth, we will be able to take our final breath in peace.

As of this writing, Nanci Alcorn, the wife of Randy Alcorn, the well-known author of *Heaven*, had just stepped into the Heaven her husband wrote about so eloquently. She courageously fought this fight for many years. In August 2021, Randy wrote, "To clarify, Nanci isn't teetering on the edge and we aren't desperately trying to cling to earthly life at the expense of its quality, rather we are taking the opportunity to improve that quality. If the time comes when God seems ready to take either of us home, we will accept that and not use every possible means to prolong life at the expense of comfort and well-being. 'To depart and be with Christ . . . is better by far.'"[10]

9. See Psalm 46.
10. Posted on CaringBridge, August 31, 2021.

EAGER TO EXIT

When Bobbie was in the final weeks of her life, the hospice doctor would come to visit. Lying on a rented hospital bed in our living room, Bobbie would look up at the physician, cup her hands on either side of her mouth, as if to shout—even though she did not have the strength to lift her voice above a loud whisper: "I want to die," she'd say. My daughters and I witnessed this. More than once.

In response, seemingly oblivious to what Bobbie had just said, the doctor would respond, "On a scale from one to ten, how are you feeling?"

Way out of character for her, Bobbie would snap at him, "I'm a ten." The doctor ignored her. Literally acting like he didn't hear what she had just said. This was not a proud moment for hospice.[11] Bobbie dubbed this man "Dr. Death." I'm not kidding.

In lovely contrast, we had the pleasure of living across the street from our primary care physician. Whenever he would visit Bobbie, Dr. David Boyer listened to her sincere pleas to help bring this odyssey to a close. He did not shame her for her eagerness to die. He only smiled, took her hand, and assured her that she was in the Lord's hands. That satisfied Bobbie's anxious spirit.

In his presence and between visits, Bobbie referred to David Boyer as "Dr. Sunshine."

---

11. Every time I've heard about hospice stepping in when folks are nearing death, witnesses to the care these terminal folks have received has been extremely positive. Hospice nurses and doctors are generally very good at what they are called to do. Our experience was not one of their finer moments.

If you haven't been in this place, some day you will. Perhaps it will be as a caregiver. Or maybe it will be you. And there is no shame in longing for an end to suffering and a desire to be with God.

BEFORE YOU

Nancy and I try to be really careful about the movies we watch. I, frankly, was a bit more liberal about cinematic pleasures than she was before we married. But willingly embracing her more careful approach, we've still found plenty of common ground. Like *Me Before You*, a powerful adaptation of a novel written by *New York Times* bestselling author Jojo Moyes.[12]

We both knew quite a bit about the premise and plot of the movie, but I wasn't ready for the emotions I would experience. In brief, the story includes a handsome and athletic young man named Will Traynor, who breaks his neck in a motorcycle accident. He's consigned to life in a wheelchair. Since Will is in need of palliative care, his pretentious mother hires an inexperienced, ordinary, unemployed waitress named Louisa Clark to care for her son.

This couple improbably falls in love, a romance that has little promise because of Will's condition, with no future—since Will has made the decision to terminate his life. Louisa sets out to show Will that life is still worth living. In the end, Will's plans succeed.

---

12. Jojo Moyes, *Me Before You* (New York: Viking, 2012).

As you can imagine, the plot gripped me. When the movie ended, I sat on our couch, weeping quietly as the credits rolled. Nancy tenderly held my hand without speaking.

Knowing my wife as I do, I was confident that the whole idea of suicide under any conditions would be anathema to her. However, here was her husband in tears over a story that clearly supported euthanasia. Finally, I gained enough composure to speak.

"I understand," I said in a whisper, referring to the movie we'd just seen. "I understand," I repeated.

In the minutes that followed, I was able to tell Nancy the whole story of Bobbie at this place in her journey. Of the harrowing experience of the visits with Dr. Death and the joy of the visits with his counterpart, Dr. Sunshine. Now having heard my unvarnished description of my own account, her tenderness settled my heart.

I'm eager to draw you into this conversation in a real and personal way. As you know, it's one thing to have a strong opinion about something, but then there are times when that opinion is yanked through the fire of reality. "Okay," someone may say, "but what does this belief look like when the pressure is on . . . when it's about you or someone you love?"

I'm sitting next to the hospital bed, offensively stationed in our beautifully decorated living room. Bobbie no longer has any interest in living. This is not a dress rehearsal for me; it's the real thing. What was I to do?

The first image that came to my mind was of the concentric circles of waves that emanate from a rock thrown into a still pond. The decision about my wife's life and death went out far beyond the little tableau of a few people sitting together.

As I have done many times since first meeting Joni Eareckson Tada in 1977, I'm pleased to turn to her again for a special kind of first-person wisdom:

> If you believe your decision is private and independent, think again. Your choice to speed up the dying process is like playing a delicate game of pick-up sticks. You carefully lift a stick, hoping not to disturb the intricate web. But just when you think you've succeeded, your independent action ends up jiggling the fragile balance and sending other sticks rolling.[13]

What a powerful—and true—metaphor.

The conversations with Dr. Death and Dr. Sunshine did not take place in a vacuum. Bobbie's life—and death—made ripples big and small, literally around the world. If I believe in life's sacredness—and I do—then the decision, even as I looked into the face of my suffering mate, was beyond us to make.

Back to Joni for a moment. She was speaking at the National Religious Broadcaster's Convention closing session in 2013 when, paying special tribute to Bobbie, she spoke of an email she had received from me.

In quoting my wife, I wrote to Joni and she read these words to those gathered:

---

13. Joni Eareckson Tada, *When Is It Right to Die? A Comforting and Surprising Look at Death and Dying*, rev. ed. (Grand Rapids: Zondervan, 2018), 71.

Just as chemo medicine is designed to kill the bad cancer cells, so God designs a toxic painful trial to destroy and starve and kill anything in my soul that is selfish, unholy, or offensive to Him. I willingly surrender to His infusion, knowing that He has chosen what will ultimately bring me more abundant life than I can ever imagine. I choose to open my hands and my heart and offer my veins to be infused with His choice of trial, so that I might receive His beauty and His perfect health.[14]

Joni also quoted from the apostle Peter's first epistle. As she often does, Joni lifts the sacred Scripture to shed light on truth: "To this you were called, because Christ suffered for you, leaving you an example, that you should follow in his steps" (1 Peter 2:21).

You may die suddenly in a car accident or from a massive heart attack, like Nancy's daddy on the tennis court in 1979. Or you may die incrementally, like Bobbie did in 2014 after thirty months of a relentless and courageous battle.

There's no need to spend much time in the former scenario. But the latter?

Can we talk?

I'm earnestly pro-life. News related to abortion on demand captures my undivided attention, perhaps more than any other issue out there. Long before the issue became a

---

14. "Joni Eareckson Tada Speaks at the 2013 NRB Convention," March 18, 2013, YouTube, www.youtube.com/watch?v=jrO5fGSIyM8. The reference to Bobbie starts at time stamp 31:15, but I commend this entire unforgettable video to you.

political volleyball—a place where it never belonged—I have steadfastly believed that human life begins at conception.[15]

"Okay, Robert," you might ask, "how does this view square with end-of-life issues. Like what you and Nancy experienced in the movie. Like what you witnessed with Bobbie, who was understandably eager to end it all?"

This question is totally fair to ask, and my response deserves far more space than the final few paragraphs of this book. Men and women—living and dead—whom I love and respect have written extensively on this subject, so I will not fill the final pages with what you can find in libraries and on internet sites. But let me take a quick run at it.

Joni, who has had every reason to end her life, is unapologetic about this, going way back to soon after she broke her neck in 1967.

She writes:

Once again, I desperately wanted to kill myself. Here I was, trapped in this canvas cocoon. I couldn't move anything except my head. Physically, I was little more than a corpse. I had no hope of ever walking again. I could never lead a normal life . . . I had absolutely no idea of how I could find purpose or meaning in just existing day after day—waking, eating, watching TV, sleeping.

---

15. This belief comes from undergraduate studies of mammals and five decades of conversations with experts and reading since. Until *Roe v. Wade* was decided by the United States Supreme Court in 1973, this belief was not limited to clergy opinion. It was a nearly unanimous belief among scientists and physicians. After *Roe*, millions took to the streets to express their opinions. Unable to speak were the approximately 63 million children whose lives were snuffed out without their consent.

Why on earth should a person be forced to live out such a dreary existence? How I prayed for some accident or miracle to kill me. The mental and spiritual anguish was as unbearable as the physical torture.[16]

Never shy about dealing honestly with this subject, Joni describes tuning into a segment of NBC's *Today Show* many years ago. The featured guest that day was Derek Humphry, the author of *Final Exit*[17] and the president of the Hemlock Society at that time.

Joni remembers one particular exchange in which Bryant Gumbel, the host of the show, lifted Humphry's book and tilted it so he could read the subtitle out loud. Joni writes that at the time of its release, "some called the book controversial; others said it should never have been published; and still others insisted bookstores should boycott it."

Gumbel looked dispassionately at Humphry and spoke: "No qualms about the possibility that this book could get into the hands of someone who is simply depressed but very curable?" Humphry responded with his typical, understated serenity, proving in that moment something you and I know full well: words mean things. He said he was *not* promoting suicide, but that dying individuals who wish to achieve a painless death ought to be allowed to plan for it.[18]

Okay, were you able to follow his logic? I wasn't either. Our old buddy Noah Webster cuts to the chase with his

---

16. Joni Eareckson Tada, *Joni: An Unforgettable Story*, 45th anniv. ed. (Grand Rapids: Zondervan, 2021), 70.
17. Derek Humphry, *Final Exit: The Practicalities of Self-Deliverance and Assisted Suicide for the Dying*, 3rd ed. (New York: Dell, 2002).
18. Recounted in Tada, *When Is It Right to Die?*, 26.

terse definition of suicide: "to intentionally end one's own life." I suppose the operative word here is *intentionally*. Whether I put a gun to my own head or direct someone to prepare a poisonous cocktail for me to drink, suicide is . . . suicide.

The kind of word salad Derek Humphry served up that morning on the *Today Show* in Joni's hearing is colloquially known as "a distinction without a difference." But these days, doesn't it seem like words spoken and posted here and there on social media are indiscriminately slapped about like worthless gnats on a summer evening?

But words—and actions—mean things. Real things.

You and I may die suddenly. Maybe a sharp, stabbing pain to our chests and the lights go out. Or maybe a swerving 18-wheeler headed directly at us on a two-lane road. Boom! Crash! We're dead.

Or our death may be incremental. Prolonged. With lots of time for us to lie quietly and think about it. Even to ponder speeding up the dying process.

When in 2020, I was diagnosed with two different, unrelated cancers and was put through all kinds of slices, sticks, and sedations, I had very little pain. Sure, a little discomfort now and then but nothing even close to deep stabbing or sustained chronic pain. But what if there had been? How would I have handled the kind of utter despair and eagerness to die that are often companions of this kind of physical treachery?

Because I have such confidence in Joni's life and work and faith in Christ, you're welcome to treat this chapter as a shameless infomercial for her seminal work *When Is It*

Right to Die? If you would like a strong biblical approach to questions you or someone you love have on issues such as euthanasia and assisted suicide, her book is exactly what you're looking for. Here are a few bullet points to whet your appetite:[19]

+ *Legalized euthanasia results in physicians being cast in the role of killer, not healer.*

    For some twenty-four hundred years, people who are terminally ill, dying, or disabled have had the assurance that doctors operate under the Hippocratic Oath, a promise to heal them, not kill them. But fewer and fewer medical schools consider this classical oath relevant. For example, the oath used by a well-known university school of medicine—a school committed to training skilled medical professionals with a commitment to Christian service—lists no objections to abortion when there are suspicions of the baby's condition and needle-threading euthanasia.

+ *Legalized euthanasia results in less care for the dying.*

    Rather than allowing doctors to provide better care, legalized euthanasia gives permission to suggest to hurting individuals that society is eager to see their death. It's a matter of economics. Euthanasia is extraordinarily cheap when compared to the costs of humane chronic and terminal care.

+ *Legalized euthanasia establishes a fundamental right to die.*

---

19. Much of the material here in this bulleted list is either reproduced verbatim or is paraphrased from Joni's *When Is It Right to Die?* (75–79).

Even with supposed safeguards written into physician-assisted suicide legislations, these laws are stacked against the patient and apply to people with years, even decades to live. Doctors make the determination that a person is terminally ill, and doctors are often wrong in predicting life expectancy.

• *Legalized euthanasia reveals that the character of a helping society is beginning to disintegrate.*

I remember so well when Francis Schaeffer was touring to promote his book *How Should We Then Live?*[20] I heard him speak to a massive crowd at the McCormick Place in Chicago. I will never forget when this whimsical-looking prophet delivered a knockout punch more lethal than his small stature and shepherd's garb would have ever imagined. He told the crowd that, primarily because of the rampant pandemic of abortion sweeping our nation but also in response to all kinds of life issues, once the life-and-death line is crossed, the question must be asked, "Who redraws it?" Except for capital punishment visited on a convicted and admitted and guilty murderer, the voluntary taking of human life will always be wrong. Always.[21]

• *Legalized euthanasia broadens the "right to die" to a right to be killed.*

Again, trafficking in Dr. Schaeffer's wisdom, this fine line becomes broader and broader as careless advocates systematically chip away at the sixth and

---

20. Frances A. Schaeffer, *How Should We Then Live?* (Old Tappan, NJ: Revell, 1976).
21. I provide my own commentary on this bullet point here.

unequivocal commandment, sent by the finger of God to stone tablets in Moses' arms: *You shall not murder.*[22]

Do you remember the heated conversation between the patriarch Jacob and his barren wife Rachel? "Give me children, or I'll die!" In anger, Jacob responded in the moment, but his words continue to ring true millennia later: "Am I in the place of God?" (Genesis 30:1–2). How dangerous, how perilous, would it be to find ourselves in this place?

What if Joni had been granted her death wish as a seventeen-year-old? Instead of dying as a teenager, Joni has been dramatically used by God in spite of those early longings to die. Her impact is worldwide. Fifty-five years later and counting.

And for Bobbie, even though she only lived a few months after her tense conversations with Dr. Death, I'm picturing a veritable parade of friends who came to visit with her those weeks. I'm hearing her prayers on their behalf, including a young man who committed his life to Jesus Christ by faith, sitting next to her hollowed-out form as she lay on the hospital bed. Standing around the corner so as not to tamper with the tenderness of the moment, I remember weeping as this frail and faithful servant ushered a successful and strong businessman, broken and repentant of his own sinfulness, thanking Jesus and inviting the Lord to save him. Some day when this man crosses over, he and Bobbie will spend eternity as friends.

---

22. Once again, this is my own commentary.

PARTING

Do you remember the balcony scene in which Juliet says goodbye to Romeo? And do you remember two disparate words that showed up side by side? "Sweet sorrow."

In August 2014, Bobbie and I rendezvoused with Joni and her husband, Ken. Without going into graphic detail, I needed a tutorial from Ken on how to navigate the leg bags that a nephrologist had just strapped to Bobbie's legs. As you can imagine, Ken was a wonderful and patient instructor.

In addition to a precious chance to spend a little time with these priceless friends, we had a chance to laugh, to reminisce, to sing, to pray, and to enjoy the luxury of being together. At one point, I pulled out my cell phone, pointed it at Joni and Bobbie, and began taking their picture.

Moments after taking the first picture, they looked at each other. I don't remember who mentioned it, but it suddenly dawned on one of them that this was likely the last time they'd be together this side of glory. At this, these two women collapsed on each other's shoulder in tears. If nothing else, the second photo was a perfect display of the idea of "sweet sorrow."

Seventy days later, Bobbie would be going ahead of Joni, crossing her own finish line. As of this writing in 2022, Joni is still gloriously rolling.

Through choked sobs and real tears, we closed out our time with Ken and Joni singing the chorus of a hymn many believers have sung down through the years, at moments just like this one:

Till we meet, till we meet,
till we meet at Jesus' feet.
Till we meet, till we meet,
God be with you till we meet again.[23]

Amen.

---

23. Jeremiah Eames Rankin, "God Be With You Till We Meet Again" (1880). Public domain.

EPILOGUE

READY

God's people should plan for a voyage of a thousand years, but be prepared to abandon ship tonight.

JOSEPH BAYLY

Even though I own a set of golf clubs, I'm far from considering myself a "golfer." When I'm asked if I play, I always qualify my yes with a realistic comment about the quality of my game. Breaking 100 and counting all the strokes is cause for serious celebration.

But even though I'm just a duffer, I do know enough about golf to be familiar with an expression I've heard golfers use when they're playing on a crowded course and have a foursome pressing in behind them. A group of eager golfers breathing down their necks.

What this looks like is that when it's time for your foursome to tee off, each golfer is prepared to step up and hit their shot. This isn't a time for dawdling. No leaning over your ball and taking your sweet time. Or after your tee shots are out there and you scatter to the fairway, the trap, the tall grass, or the forest, the person who has located their golf ball and is in place, even if it's not officially their turn, goes ahead and hits their shot.

The expression is easy to understand. Totally self-explanatory.

"Ready golf."

The United States Golf Association actually has an official definition for ready golf: "Rule 6.4 expressly allows playing out of turn in match play by agreement, and for stroke play, affirmatively allows and encourages players to play out of turn in a safe and responsible way to save time or for convenience (also known as 'ready golf')."[1]

In chapter 8, I told you about Paul Azinger's powerful, gospel-driven, and hilarious eulogy for his fallen friend Payne Stewart. Payne and two of his closest friends had perished in a tragic private plane crash. One of those friends was a man named Robert Fraley, Payne's agent. I knew Robert. In fact, a year before the accident, he and I discussed the possibility of merging our businesses. He was in the sports representation business; I was in the author representation business. And even though this transaction didn't work out, we remained friends.

In late October 1999, when we heard the news of the plane crash, Bobbie and I hurried from our home in Nashville to

1. "Major Change: Encouraging Prompt Pace of Play," USGA, accessed June 30, 2022, www.usga.org/content/usga/home-page/rules-hub/rules-modernization/major-changes/encouraging-prompt-pace-of-play.html.

Orlando. One of my closest friends, Orel Hershiser, also a Robert Fraley client, invited us to stay in his home. I will never forget what Orel said when we first saw each other. After a bear hug and some tears, Orel said of Robert, "He was ready."

For context, Robert was forty-six years old—*only* forty-six years old. A man whose reputation for relentless integrity reflected the reality of his love for Christ and his eagerness to honor Him by living and working with excellence. The last thing Robert expected that cool autumn day when he climbed aboard the Learjet 35 in Sanford, Florida, was that this would be his final day on earth. Who at such a young age and with an enviable and successful career in sports would expect that?

But as his friend, Orel, who knew him so well, said through sobs, "He was ready."

You and I have journeyed through this book together, spending several hours chatting. We've covered all kinds of things that I truly hope have been helpful as you move toward your own finish line.

Regardless of your age, you and I don't know how long we have until it's our turn to hit the tape at the end of the straightaway. But like golfers who have decided not to waste any time to take their shot as they play "ready golf," my deepest hope is that you and I will be . . . ready.

READY IS GOOD

Think back to your school days. It doesn't matter how far back you go. It could be elementary or graduate school. Junior or senior high.

When you were headed into a classroom or the room where a panel of professors are about to hear the oral defense of your doctoral dissertation, if you believed you were ready, you were at peace.

It's the confidence of striding into the sanctuary for your wedding, dressed and ready. Or sitting down at a business meeting with your research complete. This wedding and this meeting did not sneak up on you. You knew all about them with plenty of time in advance to do what you needed to do to prepare.

On the contrary, there is no sheer panic like the sheer panic of *not* being ready. This is the fluster of terror that makes breathing difficult. The sweat on your face that shouts, *I didn't do my homework. I'm not prepared for this.*

In the late 1960s, a popular West-Coast-based singer-songwriter named Larry Norman penned the words to a song with a sobering theme—the return of Jesus Christ. So fitting to the idea of this epilogue, the song was titled, "I Wish We'd All Been Ready."[2] The lyrics included the narrative of a sleeping couple, awakened by a noise that signaled the rapture—the teaching of some Christians that, in the twinkling of an eye, Jesus will come from heaven and believers who are still alive will be gathered and taken to be with the Lord in heaven (see 1 Thessalonians 4:16–17). The wife turned to ask her husband if he was able to identify what had made the noise. But because he was ready, his body was gone. His side of the bed was empty. She was not ready. He was.

There it is. Just like speeding up your golf game or

2. Larry Norman, "I Wish We'd All Been Ready" (1969) © Beechwood Music Corporation, Ordure Blanc Music, J.C. Love Pub. Co.

readying yourself for an airplane disaster, the operative word is *ready*.

One of two things waits for us in our future, regardless of our beliefs about the rapture. These two assertions are not speculation; they're fact. And we have no choice but to accept them.

The first is that, in our lifetime or later, *Jesus Christ will return to earth.* His physical, resurrected form will show up, just as He did on Christmas Eve. Back then He came as an innocent baby boy to a peasant couple. But not this time. He's not going to be a helpless, dependent newborn infant sleeping on itchy straw in a feeding trough. No, He'll look more like the apostle John describes Him in the first chapter of the book of Revelation.[3]

> The hair on his head was white like wool, as white as snow, and his eyes were like blazing fire. His feet were like bronze glowing in a furnace, and his voice was like the sound of rushing waters. In his right hand he held seven stars, and coming out of his mouth was a sharp, double-edged sword. His face was like the sun shining in all its brilliance. (Revelation 1:14–16)

Take a moment to let this image sink in. And what did John do when he witnessed this thing with his own eyes? He did what we will do when we see Jesus: "When I saw him, I fell at his feet as though dead" (Revelation 1:17a).

And what will Jesus do and say to us as we lie on our

---

3. I'll never forget the bumper sticker I saw years ago: "Jesus is coming back, and man, He's really ticked."

faces before Him? "Then he placed his right hand on me and said: 'Do not be afraid'" (Revelation 1:17b).

The apostle Paul also references this view of the Savior. He uses words we completely understand: "in a flash" and "in the twinkling of an eye."

> Listen, I tell you a mystery: We will not all sleep, but we will all be changed—in a flash, in the twinkling of an eye, at the last trumpet. For the trumpet will sound, the dead will be raised imperishable, and we will be changed. (1 Corinthians 15:51–52)

The second sure thing is that *you and I will die*—unless Christ returns before our death. We will take that final breath and our bodies will turn gray and cold. This end may come at the close of a protracted illness. In that case, for you and your loved ones it will not be a surprise.

Or it may happen like my wife Nancy's dad, Arthur DeMoss. On a clear Saturday morning on the tennis court with three of his buddies, at the age of fifty-three, my future father-in-law, whom I'm eager to meet in Heaven, suffered a massive heart attack, a lethal myocardial infarction. Doctors said he was dead before his body slammed to the hard surface of the court.

Because of the wonder of technology, as I was working on this manuscript, Nancy and I watched a DVD of her daddy's funeral service, held on September 10, 1979. Right there, sitting on the front row next to my wife at twenty-one years old, were her forty-one-year-old mother and six young siblings. Nancy's eight-year-old sister slept through much of the three-hour service.

Speakers included well-known Christian leaders and two men whom Art DeMoss had introduced to Jesus. Each speaker affirmed the relentless witness of this man's words and life. And in spite of the pain of the moment, they celebrated one simple fact: even as a young man in his fifties, Art DeMoss was ready.

Whether your death is sudden or prolonged ... or if Jesus returns before you are hit by a car or get sick, in any case, only one question matters. Only one.

Are you ready?

"HERE COMES DA JUDGE"

You may be old enough to remember the weekly comedy variety show *Rowan & Martin's Laugh-In*. It ran from 1968 to 1973 and featured many up-and-coming funny people, like Arte Johnson in a military helmet, whose oft-repeated line with a squint, curled lip, and lisp was, "Very interesting."

Remember?

Another phrase we heard almost every week on the show was the one Sammy Davis Jr.—in a white wig and black robe—uttered: "Here comes da judge." He'd speak these words as he strode across our screens. This was always good for a laugh.

But speaking of "Are we ready?" there's a biblical element of what we're going to face after death. We will be standing before the judgment seat of God, the ultimate Judge. And there will be nothing funny about it.

> THE ONLY RIGHTEOUSNESS WITH WHICH I'M JUSTIFIED IS *JESUS CHRIST'S* RIGHTEOUSNESS. BECAUSE OF JESUS, THERE'S NO REASON TO DREAD THIS JUDGMENT. THERE'S EVERY REASON TO ANTICIPATE IT.

Here's what the apostle Paul wrote about this moment: "In the presence of God and of Christ Jesus, who will judge the living and the dead, and in view of his appearing and his kingdom, I give you this charge . . . be prepared in season and out of season" (2 Timothy 4:1–2). Paul could have been talking about "ready golf," but instead he used the words "be prepared."

What that means—if you can begin to take it in—is that when you and I stand before God, we will be able to say that we are righteous before Him as His Son Jesus Christ is righteous.

When you and I know with absolute certainty that our end is near, God Himself will be our refuge. Our strength. The Lord Almighty will be with us.

How is that true? The answer is that because the only righteousness with which I'm justified is *Jesus Christ's righteousness.* More than a century and a half ago, the hymnwriter Edward Mote said it beautifully: "Dressed in His righteousness alone, faultless to stand before the throne."[4]

Because of Jesus, there's no reason to dread this judgment. There's every reason to anticipate it. How good is this?

4. Edward Mote, "The Solid Rock" (1834). Public domain.

THE PILGRIM'S PROGRESS,
A REPRISE

You may remember my telling you about how my mother, Grace, read from *The Pilgrim's Progress* to my siblings and me when we were little. The book is an allegory of a man named Christian's life journey from his birth to his death—to the vaunted Celestial City.

Even though I admit to not remembering the portion of the book that mother read about death, I have gone back and pulled out a few sentences that describe this in a way that ought to take our collective breath away.

Before arriving in this magnificent city, there was a raging river to cross. This intimidated Christian and his friend, Hopeful, but they forged ahead across the water anyway. Listen to this:

> Then they addressed themselves to the water; and entering, Christian began to sink, and crying out to his good friend, Hopeful, he said, "I sink in deep waters; the billows go over my head; all his waves go over me!" . . .
> Then said the other, "Be of good cheer, my brother, I feel the bottom, and it is good."[5]

For me, the equivalent of "feeling the bottom" is riding on an airplane as we approach a landing in dense clouds. White seamlessness out the window . . . and then, a break

---

5. John Bunyan, *The Pilgrim's Progress* (1678; repr., London: Partridge, 1870), 129.

in the whiteness and land is spotted below. I love that sight. And that feeling.

Christian felt the sandy bottom of the river with his feet, and it made him feel safe. He saw land through the clouds, and it made him happy.

That can be you and me, headed for glory. Safely.

BOBBIE WAS READY

A few months after we said goodbye to Bobbie at her funeral, I wrote the following to the many friends who had patiently and prayerfully followed our journey. My family and I had been blanketed with an outpouring of love and kindness.

Closure . . . A Final Goodbye . . . and Grateful

> The steadfast love of the LORD never ceases;
>> his mercies never come to an end;
> they are new every morning;
>> great is your faithfulness.
>> (Lamentations 3:22–23 ESV)

Precious Family and Friends:

Since my last memo to you, our family has experienced an armful of "firsts." Thanksgiving. Christmas. The New Year. Valentine's Day. Three grandchildren's birthdays. My birthday.

Many have asked how we are doing. It's a question we

have answered often. In fact, the first Sunday after Bobbie stepped into Heaven, I was on the phone with our Julie. "What should we say when people wonder how we are?" she asked.

We talked about it and reviewed several options. And then we settled on a single word. A word we have now said over and over again.

Grateful. We're grateful.

To folks who don't know Jesus, this could easily sound like we are refusing to face the facts. The painful truth that Bobbie is gone. How naive could we be? But it is true. God's faithfulness has been sure. And certain. As our Shepherd, He takes care of His own. We are truly grateful.

When Bobbie was first diagnosed, my family resolved that . . . we are not angry, we are not afraid, we are receiving this as a gift, and our highest goal is that the name of Jesus would be lifted up. Did we pray for Bobbie's healing? Yes, we did. But some of our friends—people we love very much—asked why we weren't "claiming" her healing. "Wouldn't it be God's will for someone like Bobbie to be healed?" they would lovingly inquire.

After thanking them for their care, our answer was this: "Sometimes people who love Jesus are, in fact, physically healed. And sometimes they are not."

So my family prayed about this. We asked the Lord, "What is Your will?"

His answer was clear and strong. Unmistakable. And wouldn't you know it, the answer came straight from His Word?

The Lord is not slack concerning His promise, as some count slackness, but is longsuffering toward us, not willing that any should perish but that all should come to repentance. (2 Peter 3:9 NKJV)

There it was. Our answer. God's will is that lost people repent and be found—that, as Francis Thompson wrote almost a century ago, their hearts would be captured by the "Hound of Heaven."[6]

And the reports from around the world of people being touched, inspired in their walk with Jesus as a result of Bobbie's cancer, have brought our family unspeakable joy and purpose in this journey.

The outpouring of love and care from you over these three years has been more than we could have ever anticipated. We have been sustained by your prayers.

So, thank you. Thank you for standing with me . . . with us. And thank you for your encouragement as we step out in faith, eager to see what the Lord has for us now.

We love you.

Robert

So why were we grateful?

Because even though the "goodbye" meant we would not see her again on this side of glory, Bobbie was ready.

---

6. Francis Thompson, "The Hound of Heaven," first published in the periodical *Merry England* 15, no. 87 (July 1890): 163–68.

I LOVE YOU

Like a preacher who keeps referring to "my last point in this message" but having no intention of actually coming in for a landing, I do have one more thing to mention.

I've already noted that Nancy and I have begun to notice that we attend more funerals than weddings. A lot more.

Which means that our friends are dying. This reminds me of a true story I first heard from a pastor I knew. He told the story of two elderly ministers who had been friends from seminary days. Decades of brotherhood between two men.

One day they were walking down a busy sidewalk in a large city when one of them stopped, grabbed his chest, and collapsed to the concrete below with an audible thud. The other minister quickly fell to his knees beside his friend, frantically pounding the man's chest with his fists.

Folks gathered around them to see what was going on. They heard the man on his knees calling out, in full voice. More like shouting out. At first they assumed the man was wailing in grief because of his fallen comrade. But soon they realized that he was trying to speak to his friend, now lying motionless before him.

"Don't die," the desperate man hollered. "Oh, please don't die," he repeated over and over again as he pounded on the chest of his friend.

Then he said through tears, "Please don't die until I tell you how much I love you."

This is one of the things you and I need to say every time

we speak with family members and friends. Colleagues and neighbors. Business associates and fellow church members.

It's what I'd like to say to you, since you've been my traveling companion these past several hours. And something I would encourage you to say. All the time. Because while you can, people you know need to hear it from your lips.

Say it loud. Say it with all your heart. Say it because you mean it. I'm going to say it right here instead of goodbye.

And I'm going to say it every time I have a chance, until I can speak no more.

Ready?

I love you.

ROBERT WOLGEMUTH

AND THAT'S NOT ALL

These extra pages may seem like the advertisements you and I used to see on television late at night. The word *infomercial* was created for promotions that lasted a whole lot longer than thirty or sixty seconds. And after making their relentless pitch for the product, the promoters threw in the following offer that felt almost impossible to turn down: "And that's not all."

Our "finish line" conversation is completed. Having this talk to connect has been wonderful. Thank you for the privilege of connecting with you.

But before I actually go . . . As I was doing what authors commonly refer to as "the final edit" of this manuscript, a godly man stepped into Glory. To say that Dr. Edward Hindson was a brilliant man would be the understatement of this whole book. Dr. Hindson served at Liberty University for forty-eight years, having been the dean emeritus at the school of divinity and distinguished professor of religion at the time of his death. My Nancy knew him well. I know his daughter, Linda Barrick, and her family, Andy, Jen, and Josh. For his entire adult life, Dr. Hindson studied about, wrote about, lectured about, and preached about biblical truth—including Heaven.

Since the ultimate point of this book has been to prepare you for your certain death, I wanted you to hear the words of Dr. Hindson's other daughter, Christy. Here's what she said at her daddy's service, recalling the moment he died as her family had gathered together at the hospital:

What I thought would be traumatic and difficult was the most glorious moment of my life. All of a sudden, he opened his eyes and he looked up to Heaven. His face was like it was smiling and his eyes never moved. He used to sign all his letters, "Keep looking up." And that's what he did. He kept looking up.

And for about ten minutes, we cheered like we were cheering an Olympic runner across the finish line. I can't imagine how loud it was in that ICU room. Together we shouted, 'Run, Papa, run. Go. You can do it. Go, go. Well done.' And the moment he took his last breath, instead of being sad, I was filled with the most amazing peace and joy. It was like we got to go to Heaven ourselves for a minute.

And I realized in that moment that Heaven isn't something we make up to make us feel better. It's not some delusion Christians come up with. It is real. I saw it in my dad's eyes, and I will never doubt it. And if Papa were here today to talk to all of you, he'd say, "I didn't describe it good enough. It's a whole lot better. And he'd say, "Keep looking up."[1]

---

1. The memorial service can be viewed online ("Dr. Ed Hindson Memorial Service," Thomas Road On Demand, July 7, 2022, https://watch.trbc.org/media

If my children and grandchildren have a story like this to say at my funeral, that will be good. Very good.

We are confident, I say, and would prefer to be away from the body and at home with the Lord. (2 Corinthians 5:8)

/t/1_w0b5o32p). Christy's eulogy begins at time stamp 38:32. By the way, in chapter 7, I talk about giving your children and grandchildren a blessing. Dr. Hindson was a world-class "blesser." When you listen to this, you'll see what I mean. After Christy, her sister Linda's eulogy begins at 1:00:07. When you take the time to watch these tributes, you will be blown away. And blessed. I promise.

WITH GRATITUDE

In 1957, my dad, a car-loving guy, took me to a Chevrolet assembly plant in St. Louis, Missouri. I don't remember who else went with us, but I will never forget watching with wonder how a car is put together. You may know that at the beginning, a modest-looking chassis starts its journey down the line, riding on its own wheels.

Then, seemingly out of midair, an engine block descends, soon being lowered into place. Back then, there were actual human workers all the way along, making certain pieces and parts are properly seated. Today, robots have rudely—but efficiently—replaced many of the line workers. As the evolving vehicle travels along, things are added—the main body, fenders, window glass, interior upholstery, and so forth. When it's completely assembled, a car rolls out to a waiting truck or railcar for its trip home—and if you're lucky, to your garage.

Assembling a book can be similar to this. The raw idea is that we begin with a naked chassis, and as it moves along, things are added. Material from the author's archives and conversations with friends and experts gets added. Sometimes excerpts from other published works are harvested.

On the heels of my book about running the final circle around the track, *Gun Lap: Staying in the Race with Purpose,* *Finish Line: Dispelling Fear, Finding Peace, and Preparing for the End of Your Life* was the right next book. That was the start. I dug into my own archives and researched the topic from authors and experts who had written on the subject. I've talked about these throughout the book and identified many in the bibliography. My thanks go out to each one, living and not living.

Once the assembly was underway—and with the help of my incredible agents, Erik Wolgemuth, Austin Wilson, and Andrew Wolgemuth—a publisher was secured. Because I've been in the publishing industry longer than Fred Flintstone worked in the stone quarry in the town of Bedrock, old friends at HarperCollins Christian Publishing raised their hands and took on this project. I am grateful for the likes of Mark Schoenwald, Don Jacobson, Webb Younce, and Carolyn McCready who have been a part of this adventure from the beginning. Along the way, my old and trusted friend Dirk Buursma assumed the job of editing. Lots of back and forth with Dirk helped to polish what had been drafted. His colleagues Amanda Halash and Abby Watson also pitched in with their sharp, red pencils. I am grateful for each of these gifted assemblers.

While the editors are doing their thing, gifted marketers and publicists jump in. For the launching of this book, my sincere thanks go to Alicia Kasen and Sarah Falter.

Throughout the manuscript, I mention the funerals Nancy and I have attended or livestreamed over the past few years. Those who have "gone before us" have set the bar high.

Often, when I'm listening to a eulogy, I think to myself, *Man, I want to leave that kind of legacy.* So without naming these people, whose specific identities are not necessary to mention, I will forever be in their debt. Thank you for doing the hard work of living well. I look forward to thanking you in person someday.

The book names certain friends whom I refer to as my "pallbearers"—my attorneys, Nader Baydoun, Lisa Hagenauer-Ward; my physician, Lowell Hamel; my long-time pastor, David Swanson; my accountant, Jack Goldstein; and my financial planners, Bruce Johnson and Kris Zielstra. These professionals have provided a safety net that gave me the luxury of not having to think about the service they provide so I can trust—and sometimes completely ignore—them.

In spite of an incredibly busy schedule, Joni Eareckson Tada agreed to write the foreword. As you know if you've read through this book, her life and witness were a singular inspiration. Her friendship since 1976 has been a priceless gift. Her husband, Ken, is a treasure.

My parents, Sam and Grace Wolgemuth, decided to have six children. I'm the fourth in birth order. These five siblings have been rock-solid friends for as long as we can remember. Their mates have been wonderfully grafted in. Thanks to the wonders of technology, we're able to text thread each other. Almost every day. Thank you to Ruth, Stan, Sam, Mary Gayle, Ken, Sharon, Debbie, Dan, and Mary for their gift of friendship, in celebration of our common DNA and connective tissue.

The courage that my late wife, Bobbie, lived as she walked this road to Heaven, showing the way and, in doing so, all but eliminating the fear I may have experienced as I have thought about my own death. I have said this many times, but "Bobbie showed us exactly how to die. With grace." Thank you, Bobbie.

My daughters, Missy and Julie, who braved the precarious trail of watching their mother die, have been my companions in dealing with the awful reality of death. For the remainder of my life here on earth, I will be in their debt for their seamless wisdom and love and support. This includes their incomparable, faithful husbands, Jon and Christopher, and their precious children—Abby (and her husband Ben and their son Ezra), Luke, Isaac, Harper, and Ella.

Of course, being the mate of an author is a calling unto itself. Nancy and I are this to each other. Evenings (for her) and mornings (for me) are often lived in solo. And for friends who ask us to go out and play, we hear ourselves saying, "We'd love to go to dinner with you guys, but we're hunkered down with book deadlines." My sincere apologies and thanks go to these friends—assuming they still are. Thank you, Nancy Leigh, my lady, my love, my darling, my sweetheart . . . my friend, for your love and support in the crafting of this book and for the way you have been, in every way imaginable, the Lord's gracious blessing in my life.

Nancy and I are part of a little confab of Michiganders who meet every once in a while, but with seamless support for each other, even when we're not meeting. We call this group "Old Friends"—Byron and Sue Paulus, Martin and Helen Jones, Steve and Debby Canfield, Dave and Jeannette Cooke, Ryan and Mal Loveing. Thank you for being our friends.

Finally, and not by any stretch, less important than all of the above, I'm grateful for a Good Shepherd. Jesus is my Savior. My hope. My security. A carpenter by trade, he has promised an eternal dwelling place built for me when I die and for all the precious people I've mentioned here—and all the others I may have forgotten. I'm expecting a huge family room with comfortable furniture where we can gather and celebrate—forever. I love you.

BIBLIOGRAPHY

BOOKS I READ AND REFERRED TO IN THE WRITING OF *FINISH LINE*

Alcorn, Randy. *Heaven*. Carol Stream, IL: Tyndale, 2004.

Butler, Kathryn. *Between Life and Death: A Gospel-Centered Guide to End-of-Life Medical Care*. Wheaton, IL: Crossway, 2019.

Butler, Katy. *The Art of Dying Well: A Practical Guide to a Good End of Life*. New York: Scribner, 2020.

Gawande, Atul. *Being Mortal: Medicine and What Matters in the End*. New York: Picador, 2014.

Habecker, Hal. *What the Bible Says about Growing Older: The Exciting Potential for This Season of Life*. Plano, TX: Finishing Well Ministries, 2019.

Keller, Timothy. *On Death*. New York: Penguin, 2020.

Lutzer, Erwin W. *One Minute after You Die*. Chicago: Moody, 2015.

———. *The Vanishing Power of Death: Conquering Your Greatest Fear*. Chicago: Moody, 2004.

McCullough, Matthew. *Remember Death: The Surprising Path to Living Hope*. Wheaton, IL: Crossway, 2018.

Mitford, Jessica. *The American Way of Death Revisited*. New York: Vintage, 2000.

Moll, Rob. *The Art of Dying: Living Fully into the Life to Come*. Downers Grove, IL: InterVarsity, 2010.

Moore, Pamela Rosewell. *The Five Silent Years of Corrie Ten Boom*. Grand Rapids: Zondervan, 1986.

Packer, J. I. *Finishing Our Course with Joy: Guidance from God for Engaging with Our Aging*. Wheaton, IL: Crossway, 2014.

Sparks, David. *A Good Ending: A Compassionate Guide to Funerals, Pastoral Care, and Life Celebrations*. Toronto: United Church Publishing House, 2014.

Strobel, Lee. *The Case for Heaven: A Journalist Investigates Evidence for Life after Death*. Grand Rapids: Zondervan, 2021.

Sweeting, Donald W., and George Sweeting. *How to Finish the Christian Life: Following Jesus in the Second Half*. Chicago: Moody, 2012.

Tada, Joni Eareckson. *When Is It Right to Die? A Comforting and Surprising Look at Death and Dying*. Updated Edition. Grand Rapids: Zondervan, 2018.

Yancey, Philip. *Where the Light Fell: A Memoir*. New York: Convergent, 2021.

BIBLE TRANSLATIONS

The following Bible translations have been quoted from in this book. The permission statements for the use of the various Bible versions have been provided by their respective publishers.

◆ ◆ ◆

From the Publisher

GREAT BOOKS

ARE EVEN BETTER WHEN THEY'RE SHARED!

Help other readers find this one

- Post a review at your favorite online bookseller

- Post a picture on a social media account and share why you enjoyed it

- Send a note to a friend who would also love it—or better yet, give them a copy

Thanks for reading!